Mel Bay Presents

AUTOHARPING THE GOSPELS

By Carol Stober

1 2 3 4 5 6 7 8 9 0

Contents

Introduction

Welcome to *Autoharping the Gospels.*

This is an extension of *Flatpickin' the Gospels* by Steve Kaufman, and a recording of the music in this book is available with guitar back-up. The Autoharp arrangements were written by Carol Stober to make it easy for you to learn these great gospel tunes.

You can play chords along with the recording and/or sing, or you can play melody by following the tablature at your own pace, or with the recording. The arrangements are written as simply as possible to facilitate sight reading, so that you do not have to memorize the tune in order to play up to tempo. The publisher strongly recommends the use of the recording along with the text to insure accuracy of interpretation and ease in learning. Also sometimes it is more enjoyable to play along with accompaniment than to play alone.

I love gospel music and many of my students share a similar interest. These arrangements are for me and them, and for you.

Have fun with this book and write to me at Box 1275, Talladega, AL 35161, if you have any questions.

Sincerely,
Carol Stober

Practice Tips For Using The Gospel Duet Recording

1. Most tunes are played 3 times on the recording by guitarist, Steve Kaufman. First time through, play only the chords below the Autoharp tab line using a rhythm strum pattern. Once rhythm is established, then try playing the chords above the Autoharp tab line for melody on the 2nd or 3rd verse. Remember that when another instrument is playing lead, and the tempo is very fast, or if learning a new tune, it is proper to just play rhythm chords.

2. *The Old Rugged Cross* and *Just a Closer Walk With Thee* are played two times. *Old Time Religion* is played six times. *Old Gospel Ship* is played three and one-half times and *The Unclouded Day* is played four times through on the recording.

3. Slower tempo songs are easier to play along with. Some of these are: *Life's Railway to Heaven, Nearer My God To Thee, Faith Of Our Fathers, Near The Cross, Softly and Tenderly, What A Friend, Sweet Hour of Prayer,* and *Precious Memories.*

4. The last sentence in a song is sometimes repeated at the end. It is called a Tag. Songs on the recording with Tags are: *Nearer My God To Thee, The Lily Of The Valley, Where The Soul Never Dies, When The Saints Go Marching In, What A Friend, The Unclouded Day, Old Time Religion, The Old Rugged Cross, Heaven's Jubilee, Just A Closer Walk With Thee, A Beautiful Life,* and *Life's Railway To Heaven.*

5. Notice that often if there is no tag on a song, it begins to slow in tempo in the final measures on the recording, providing a signal that the end of the tune is approaching.

6. *Are You Washed In The Blood* is the only song in the book that needs to be transposed to another key if you play it along with the recording. The guitar has been raised two half steps to the key of A by a capo. All G's must be played on autoharp as A's. All C's are played as D's, and all D's change to E7's.

7. If a substituted melody chord sounds discordant with the recording, try to pinch a string corresponding to the melody note, and use a small pinch to avoid unwanted pitches sounding.

8. Pick-up notes (first measure) are played in the last measure when a verse is repeated two, three, or more times. To get into a song easily, listen for the pick-up notes and begin playing along at the second measure.

9. Memorize two or three favorite tunes just for the "fun of it."

About the Authors

Carol Stober is a multi-instrumental musician, entertainer, teacher, and recording artist. Her music covers a broad range of styles including bluegrass, country, folk, traditional mountain music, and gospel.

She has taught Autoharp workshops, judged Autoharp competitions at major festivals, performed at festivals, museums, churches, country music theaters, theme parks, and is an Alabama solo arts council artist conducting residencies in public schools. She was on the staff of the Old Town School of Folk Music in Chicago, Illinois, from 1980-83, and continued teaching private students since then, upon relocating in Alabama.

She graduated from the University of Maryland in 1972 with a B.S. in Secondary Education. Carol served on the Advisory Board of *The Autoharpoholic* Magazine and contributed articles for publication in it, as well as *The Autoharp Quarterly*, and *Autoharp Clearinghouse Publications*.

Carol has recorded 3 albums with Autoharp. They are *Patchwork*, *Country Sampler*, and *Rebekah, Down Home Family Band*. Her instructional titles include a book-tape Autoharp instruction set published by Workshop Records of Austin, Texas, and two Autoharp instruction videos, *Melodic Autoharp* and *Beginning Autoharp* published by Texas Music and Video Co., Levelland, Texas, and distributed by Mel Bay Publications.

Steve Kaufman is the only three-time winner of the prestigious National Flatpicking championships held in Winfield, Kansas. His music covers a broad range of styles including bluegrass favorites, popular swing standards, Irish and Appalachian fiddle tunes, folk and country classics and novelty songs. Steve has been pleasing crowds from California to Austria since 1976, performing a wide variety of acts from educational shows in elementary schools through colleges, to major bluegrass festivals, concerts and television appearances.

Steve keeps busy with his instructional books for Mel Bay Publications, audio and video instructional material for Homespun Tapes, his extensive recording career, his performance and workshop touring agenda and his Maryville private student schedule.

Some of Steve's instructional titles are *Championship Flatpicking*; *The Complete Flatpicking Book*; *Flatpickin' The Gospels*; *Bluegrass Guitar Solos That Every Parking Lot Picker Should Know—Volumes 1, 2 and 3*; *Learning To Flatpick*; and *Easy Gospel Guitar*. More titles will be coming out soon.

Understanding the Tablature System

Short, upward thumb stroke λ

Slow, long thumb stroke

Downward stroke with one finger $\downarrow$

Pluck with thumb or finger $\bigcirc$

Pinch with thumb and middle finger simultaneously $\times$

All actions must be completed in one count

For melody playing use all chords above the Autoharp tablature. For rhythm playing while singing use chords below the Autoharp tablature (i.e., guitar chords).

If the location of the 5/7 chord is easier to reach, since the chord arrangements on various Autoharps are not standard, you may substitute it for the 5 chord in most songs.

For rhythm playing use $\times \downarrow \lambda \downarrow$ for 4/4 and $\times \downarrow \lambda$ for 3/4 time songs, and ignore tab.

"Autoharp" is a registered trademark of Oscar Schmidt, Int., Chicago, Illinois. The tablature system was developed by Becky Blackley, Brisbane, California.

Understanding the Notation & Tab Examples

1) & 2)

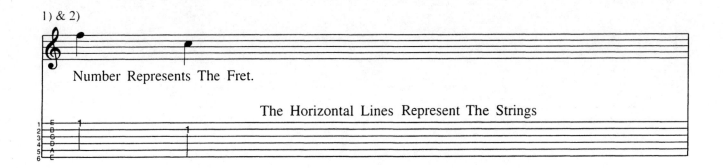

Number Represents The Fret.

The Horizontal Lines Represent The Strings

3) Quarter Notes 4) Eighth Notes

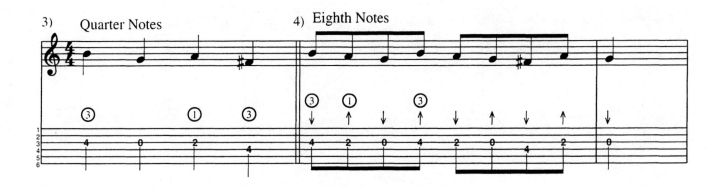

5) Half Notes Dotted Half Note Whoie Note

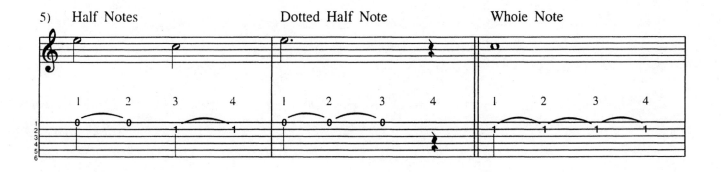

6) 1 Beat Rest 2 Beat Rest 4 Beat Rest

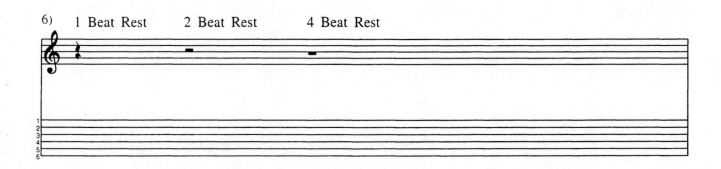

7) Hammer Ons

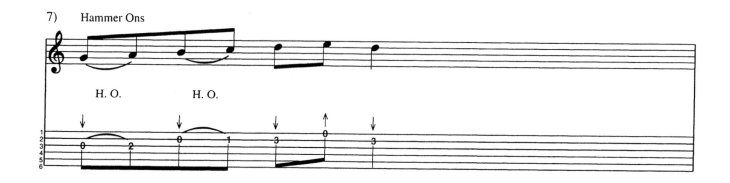

8) Slide   9) Pull Off

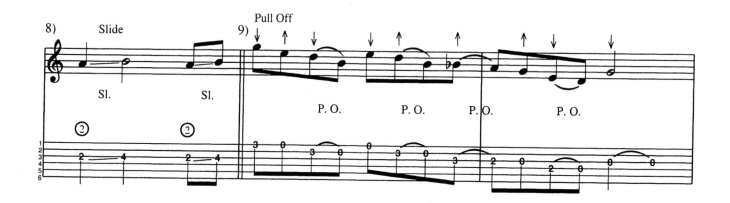

When The Roll Is Called Up Yonder

James M. Black

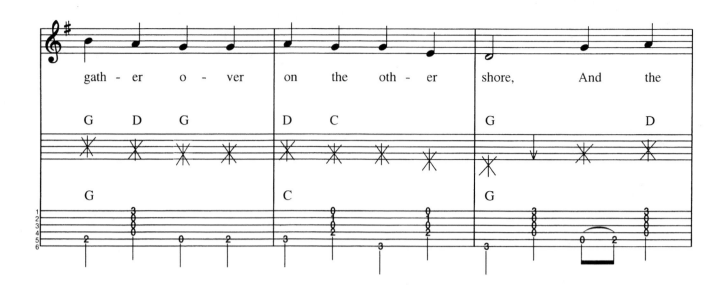

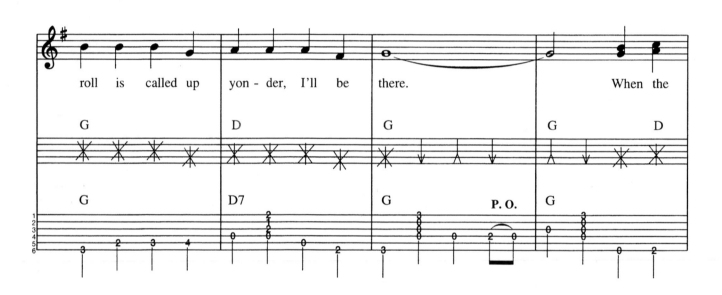

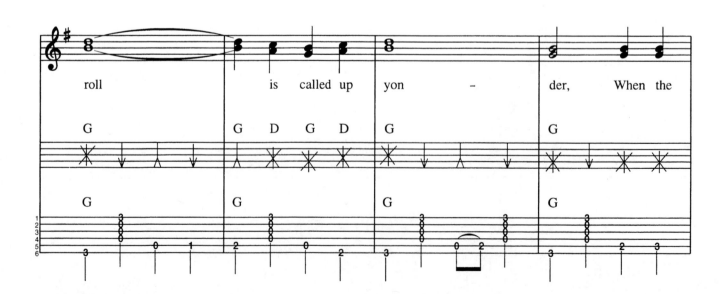

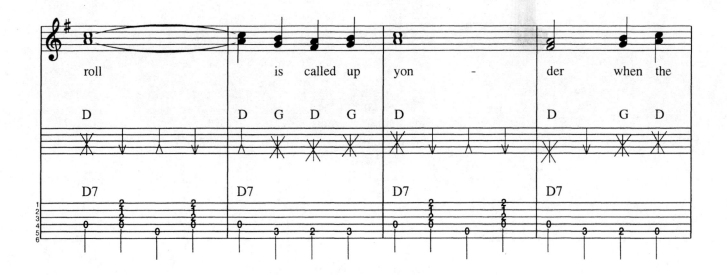

roll   is called up yon -   der when the

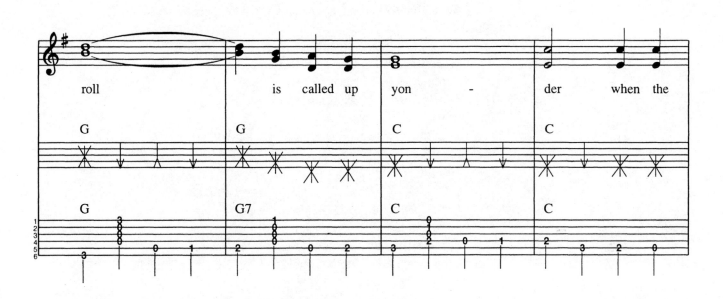

roll   is called up yon -   der when the

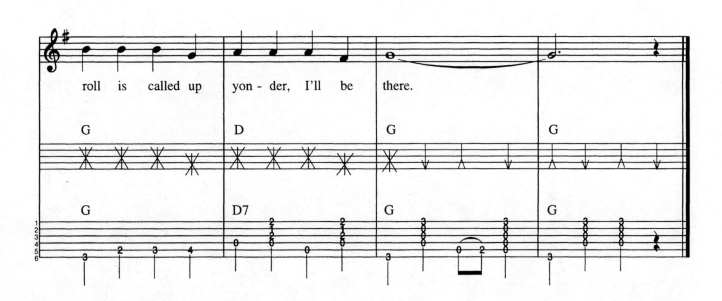

roll is called up yon - der, I'll be there.

When The Roll Is Called Up Yonder

1.   When the trumpet of the Lord shall sound,
       and time shall be no more,
       And the morning breaks eternal, bright and fair,
       When the saved of earth shall gather
       over on the other shore.
       And the roll is called up yonder I'll be there.

CHORUS

       When the roll is called up yonder.
       When the roll is called up yonder.
       When the roll is called up yonder.
       When the roll is called up yonder, I'll be there.

2.   On the bright and cloudless morning
       when the dead in Christ shall rise,
       And the glory of His resurrection share,
       When His chosen ones shall gather
       to their home beyond the skies,
       And the roll is called up yonder I'll be there.

       CHORUS

3.   Let us labor for the Master
       from the dawn till setting sun,
       Let us talk of all His wondrous love and care,
       Then when all of life is over
       and our work on earth is done,
       And the roll is called up yonder I'll be there.

       CHORUS

*This page has been
left blank to avoid
awkward page turns*

The Glory-Land Way

J. S. Torbett

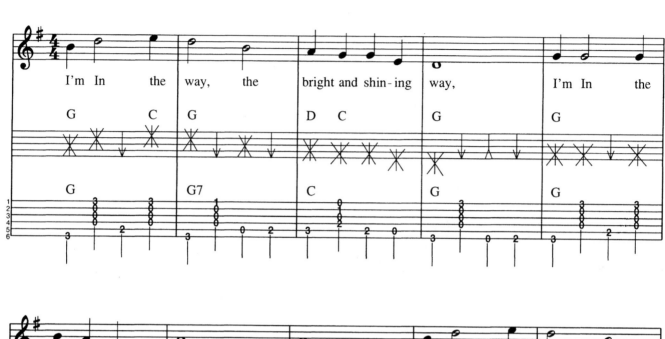

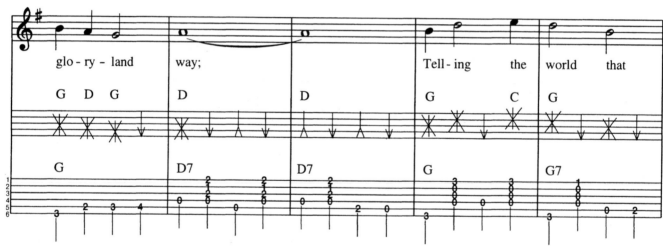

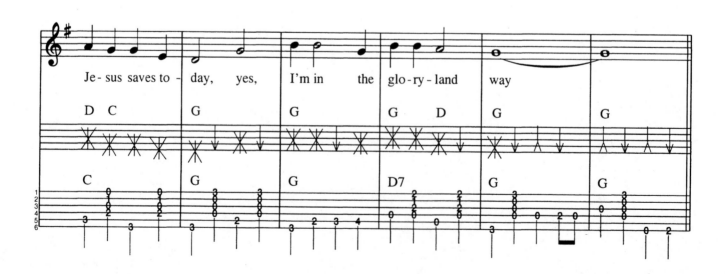

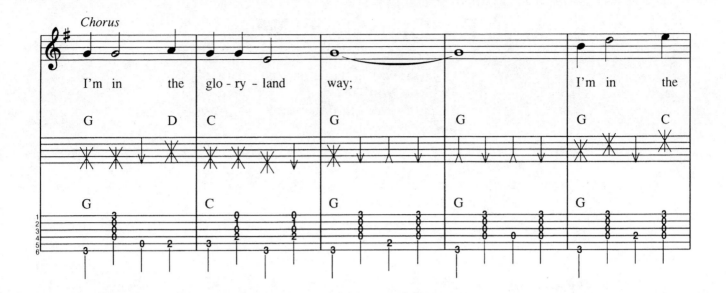

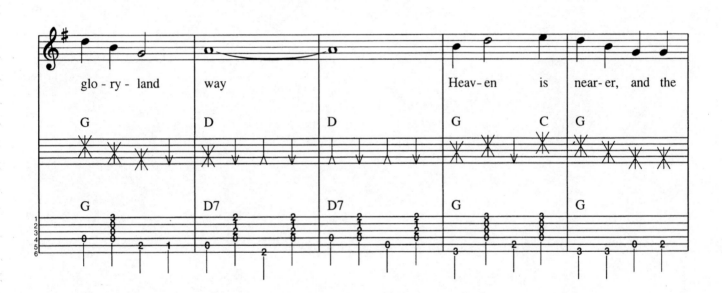

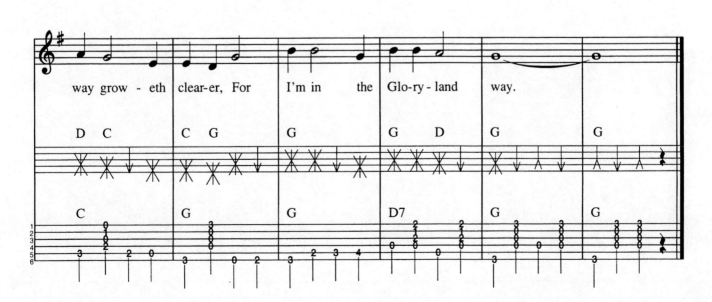

The Glory-Land Way

1. I'm in the way, the bright and shining way,
    I'm in the glory land way,
    Telling the world that Jesus saves today, Yes,
    I'm in the glory land way.

CHORUS

    I'm in the glory land way;
    I'm in the glory land way;
    Heaven is nearer, and the way grows clearer,
    For I'm in the glory land way.

2. Listen to the call, the gospel call today,
    Get in the glory land way;
    Wand'rers, come home, oh, hasten to obey,
    and get in that glory land way.

  CHORUS

3. Onward I go, rejoicing in His love,
    I'm in the glory land way;
    Soon I shall see Him in that land above,
    Oh, I'm in the glory land way.

  CHORUS

Life's Railway To Heaven

Charles D. Tillman

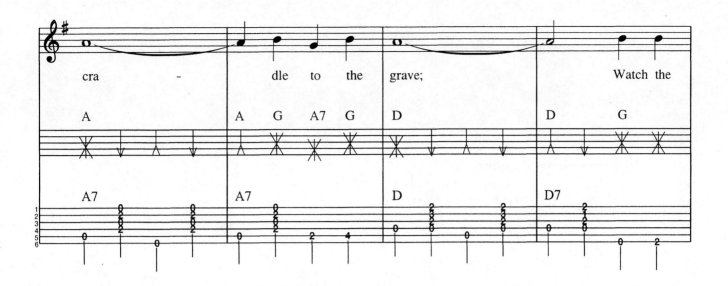

cra - dle to the grave; Watch the

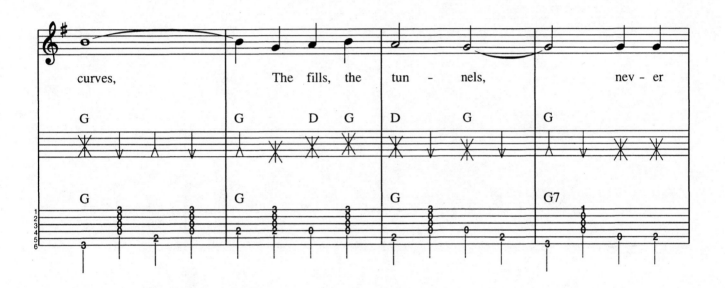

curves, The fills, the tun - nels, nev - er

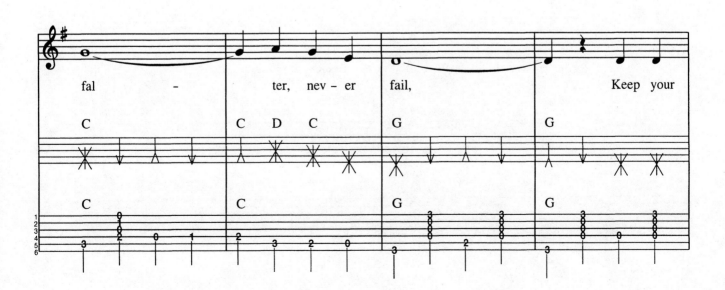

fal - ter, nev - er fail, Keep your

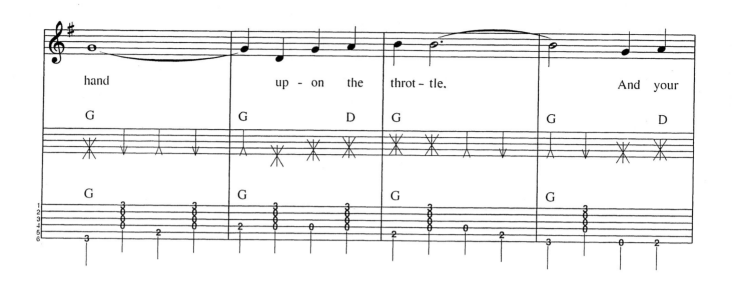

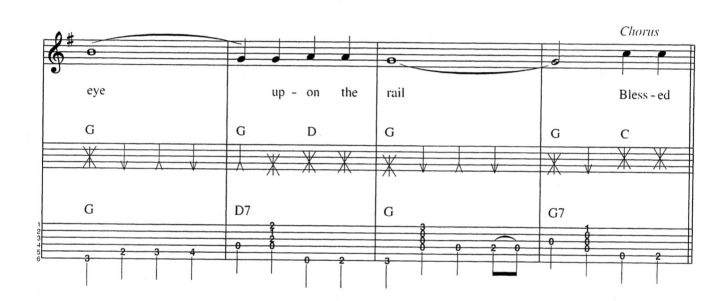

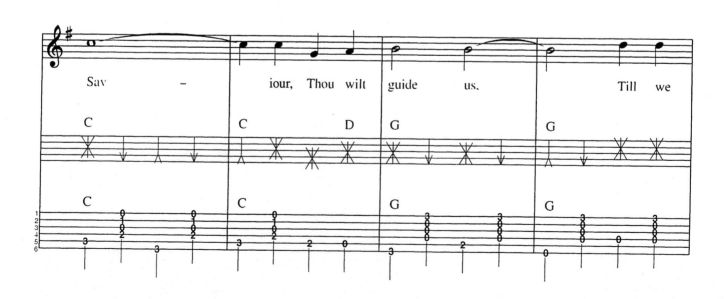

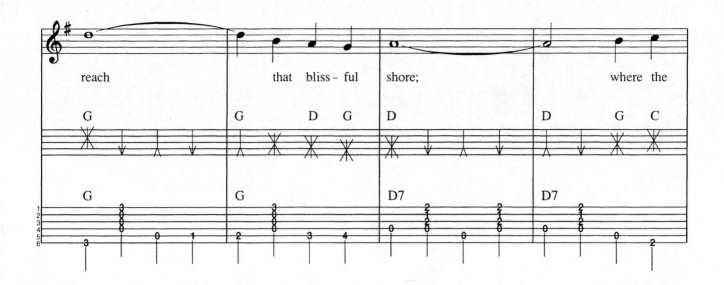

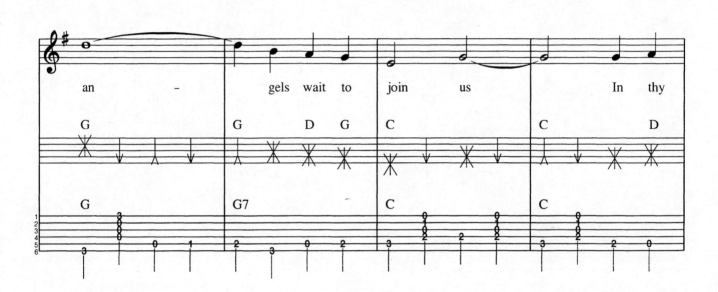

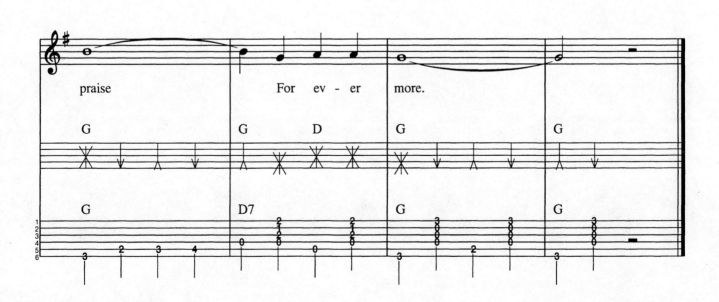

Life's Railway To Heaven

1. Life is like a mountain railroad,
   With an engineer that's brave;
   We must make the run successful,
   From the cradle to the grave;
   Watch the curves the fills, the tunnels;
   Never falter, never fail;
   Keep your hand upon the throttle,
   And your eyes upon the rail.

CHORUS

   Blessed saviour, Thou wilt guide us,
   Till we reach that blissful shore;
   Where the angels wait to join us
   In Thy praise forever more.

2. You will roll up grades of trial;
   You will cross the bridge of strife;
   See that Christ is your conductor
   On this light 'ning train of life;
   Always mindful of obstruction,
   Do your duty, never fail;
   Keep your hand upon the throttle,
   And your eyes upon the rail.

CHORUS

3. You will often find obstructions;
   Look for storms of wind and rain;
   On a fill, or curve, or trestle,
   They will almost ditch your train;
   Put your trust alone in Jesus;
   Never falter, never fail;
   Keep your hand upon the throttle,
   And your eyes upon the rail.

CHORUS

4. As you roll across the trestle,
   Spanning Jordan's swelling tide,
   You behold the Union depot
   In to which your train will glide;
   There you'll meet the Superintendent,
   God the Father, God the Son,
   With the hearty, joyful plaudit,
   "Weary pilgrim, welcome home."

CHORUS

Are You Washed In The Blood?

E. A. Hoffman

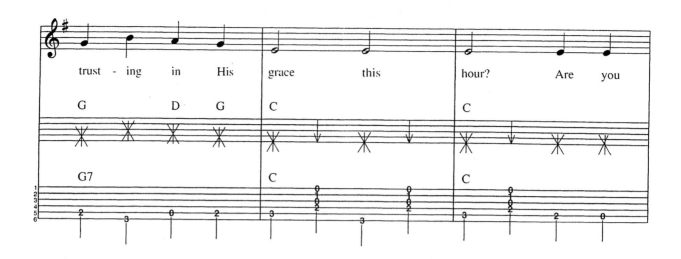

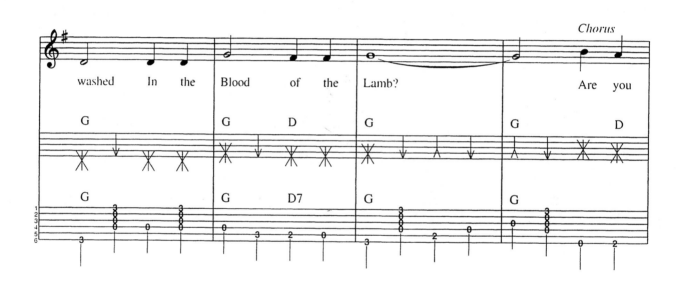

Chorus

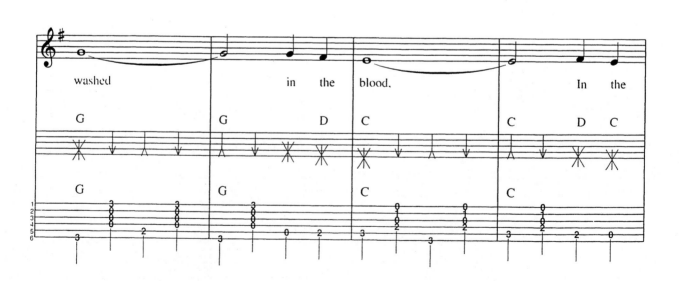

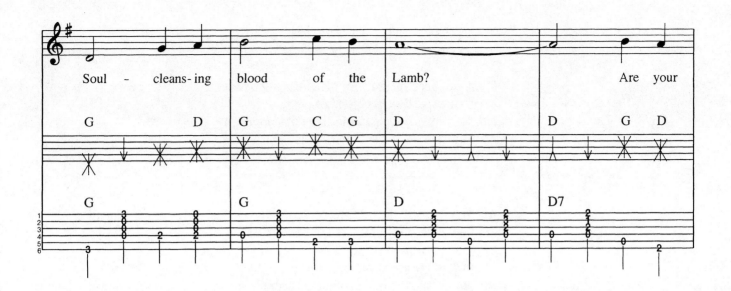

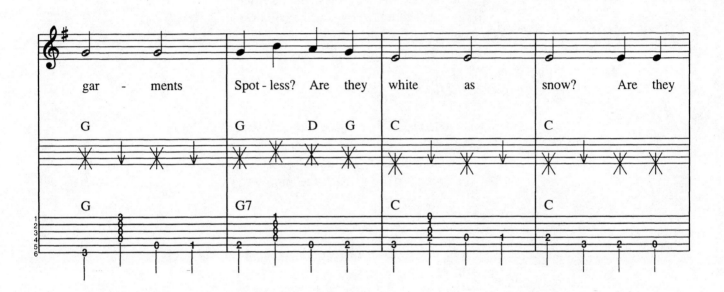

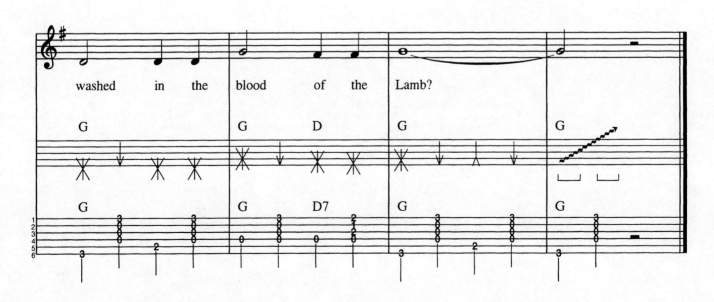

Are You Washed In The Blood?

1.   Have you been to Jesus for the cleansing pow'r?
                Are you washed in the blood of the lamb?
                Are you fully trusting in his grace this hour?
                Are you washed in the blood of the lamb?

CHORUS

                Are you washed in the blood,
                In the soul cleansing blood of the lamb?
                Are your garments spotless?
                Are they white as snow?
                Are you washed in the blood of the lamb?

2.   Are you walking daily by the saviour's side?
                Are you washed in the blood of the lamb?
                Do you rest each moment in the crucified?
                Are you washed in the blood of the lamb?

CHORUS

3.   When the Bridegroom cometh with your robes be white?
                Pure and white in the blood of the lamb.
                Will your soul be ready for the mansions bright?
                And be washed in the blood of the lamb.

CHORUS

4.   Lay aside the garments that are stained with sin,
                And be washed in the blood of the lamb?
                There's a fountain flowing for the souls unclean,
                O be washed in the blood of the lamb!

CHORUS

This page has been
left blank to avoid
awkward page turns

Nearer, My God, To Thee

Sarah F. Adams
Lowell Mason

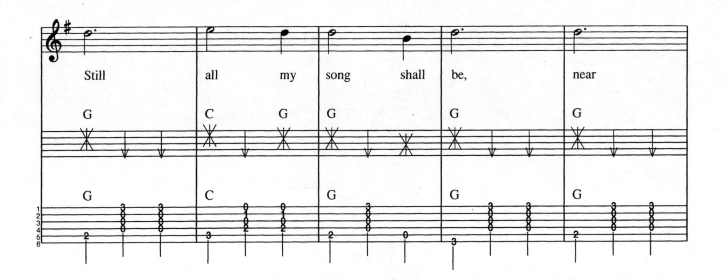

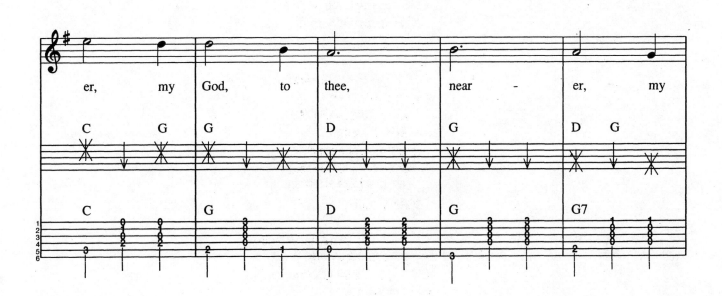

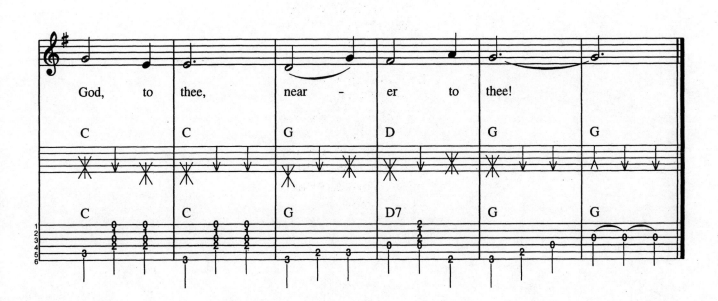

Nearer, My God, To Thee

1.   Nearer, my God, to thee,
Nearer to thee!
E'en though it be a cross
That raiseth me;
Still all my song shall be,
Nearer, my God, to thee,
Nearer, my God, to thee,
Nearer to thee!

2.   Though like the wanderer,
The sun gone down,
Darkness be over me,
My rest a stone;
Yet in my dreams I'd be
Nearer, my God, to thee,
Nearer, my God, to thee,
Nearer to thee!

3.   There let the way appear,
Steps unto heaven:
All that thou sendest me,
In mercy given:
Angels to beckon me
Nearer, my God, to thee,
Nearer, my God, to thee,
Nearer to thee!

4.   Then with my waking thoughts
Bright with Thy praise,
Out of my stony griefs
Bethel I'll raise;
So by my woes to be
Nearer, my God, to thee,
Nearer, my God, to thee,
Nearer to thee!

5.   Or if on joyful wing,
Cleaving the sky,
Sun, moon and stars forgot,
Upward I fly,
Still all my song shall be,
Nearer, my God, to thee,
Nearer, my God, to thee,
Nearer to thee!

*This page has been
left blank to avoid
awkward page turns*

Faith Of Our Fathers

H. F. Hemy
Frederick W. Faber

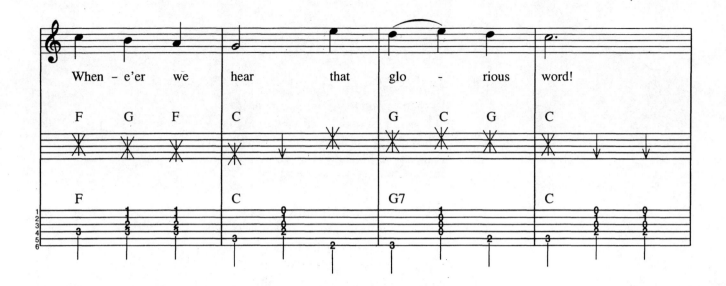

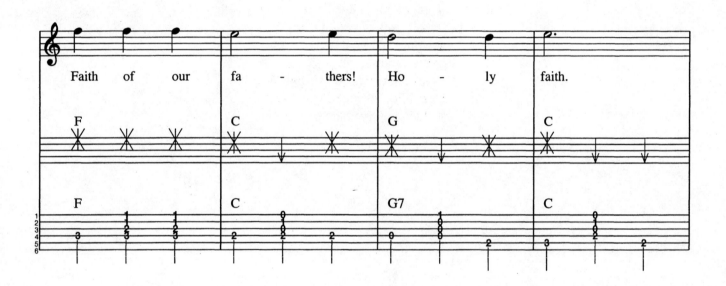

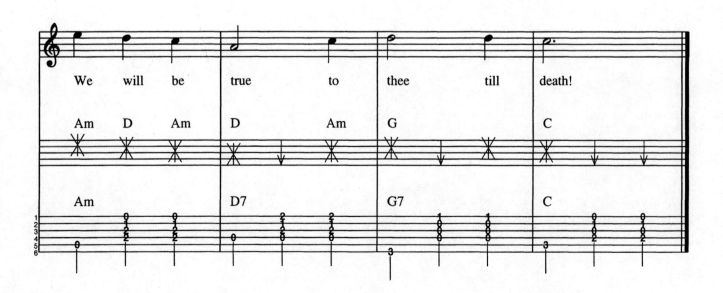

Faith Of Our Fathers

1.   Faith of our fathers! Living Still
        In spite of dungeon, fire and sword;
        O how our hearts beat high with joy
        When e'er we hear that glorious word!
        Faith of our Fathers! Holy Faith!
        We will be true to thee till death!

2.   Our fathers, chained in prisons dark,
        were still in heart and conscience free:
        How sweet would their children's fate,
        If they, like them, could die for thee!
        Faith of our Fathers! Holy Faith!
        We will be true to thee till death!

3.   Faith of our Fathers! We will love both
        friend and foe in all our strife:
        and preach thee, too,
        as love knows how,
        by kindly words and virtuous life:
        Faith of our Fathers! Holy Faith!
        We will be true to thee till death!

Blank page

*This page has been
left blank to avoid
awkward page turns*

Near The Cross

Fanny J. Crosby
W. H. Doane

36

Chorus

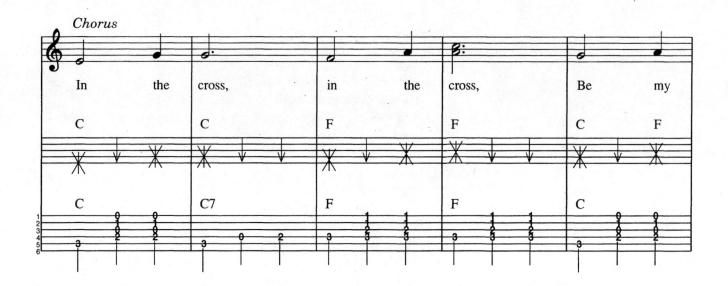

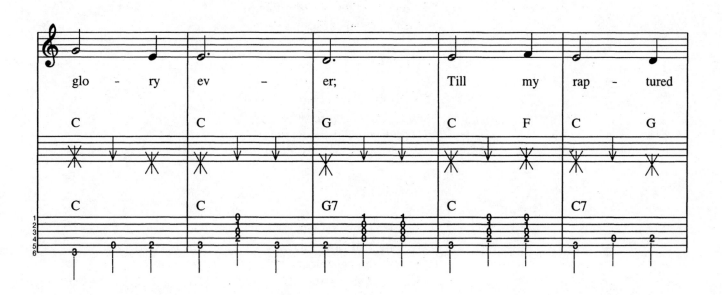

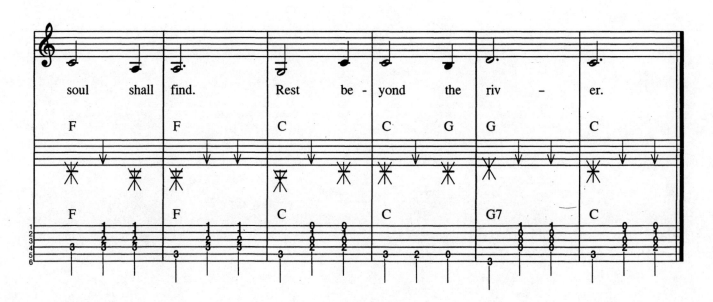

Near The Cross

1.   Jesus keep me near the cross,
There a precious fountain
Free to all a healing stream,
Flows from Calv'ry's mountain.

CHORUS

In the cross, in the cross
Be my glory ever;
Till my raptured soul shall find
Rest beyond the river.

2.   Near the cross, a trembling soul,
Love and mercy found me;
There a Bright and Morning Star
Sheds its beams around me.

CHORUS

3.   Near the cross! O lamb of God,
Bring its scenes before me;
Help me walk from day to day,
With its shadow o'er me.

CHORUS

4.   Near the cross I'll watch and wait,
Hoping, trusting ever,
Till I reach the golden strand,
Just beyond the river.

CHORUS

Softly and Tenderly

"Come unto me" - Matt. 11:28

W. L. Thompson

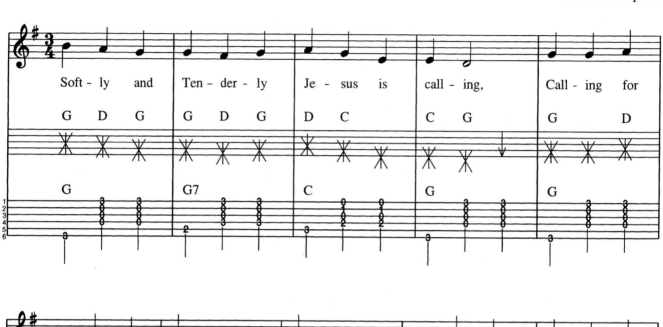

Soft - ly and Ten - der - ly Je - sus is call - ing, Call - ing for

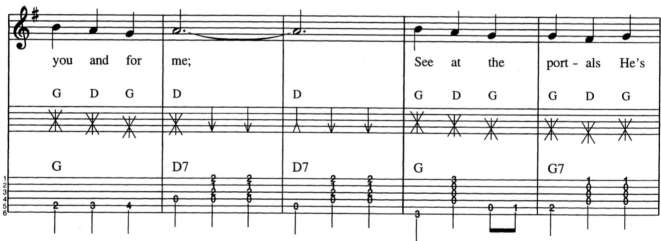

you and for me; See at the port - als He's

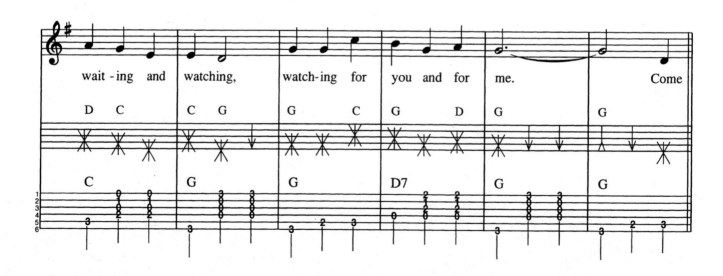

wait - ing and watching, watch-ing for you and for me. Come

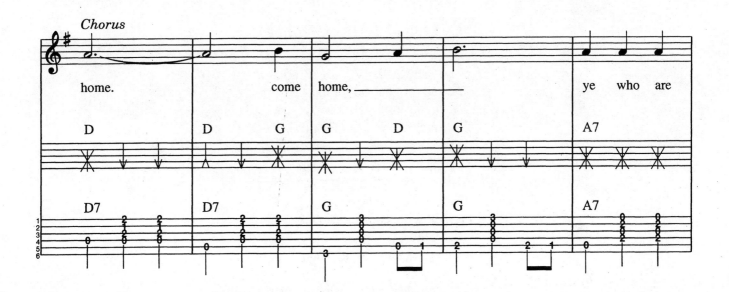

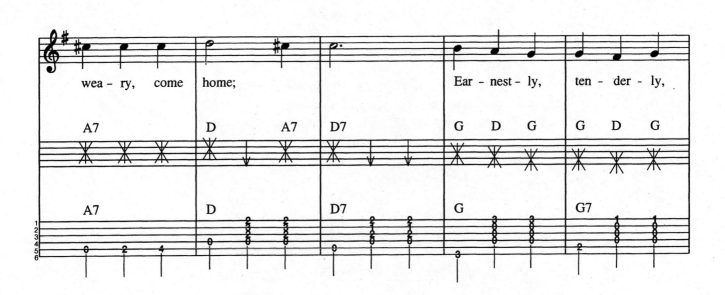

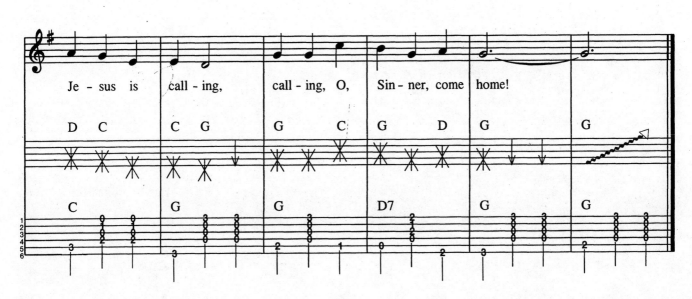

41

Softly And Tenderly

1.   Softly and tenderly Jesus is calling,
      Calling for you and for me;
      See at the portals He's waiting and watching,
      Watching for you and for me.

CHORUS

      Come home, come home, ...
      Ye who are weary, come home;
      Earnestly, tenderly, Jesus is calling,
      Calling, O, sinner, come home!

2.   Why should we tarry when Jesus is pleading,
      Pleading for you and for me?
      Why should we linger and heed not His mercies,
      Mercies for you and for me?

CHORUS

3.   Time is now fleeting, the moments are passing,
      Passing from you and from me;
      Shadows are gathering, death-beds are coming,
      Coming for you and for me.

CHORUS

4.   O for the wonderful love He has promised,
      Promised for you and for me;
      Tho' we have sinned, he has mercy and pardon,
      Pardon for you and for me.

CHORUS

The Lily Of The Valley

"A friend Loveth at all Times." Pro. 17:17

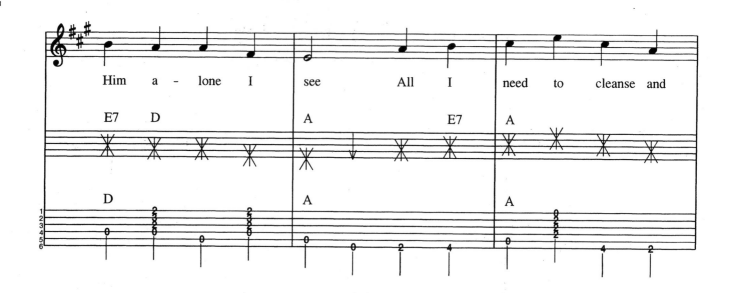

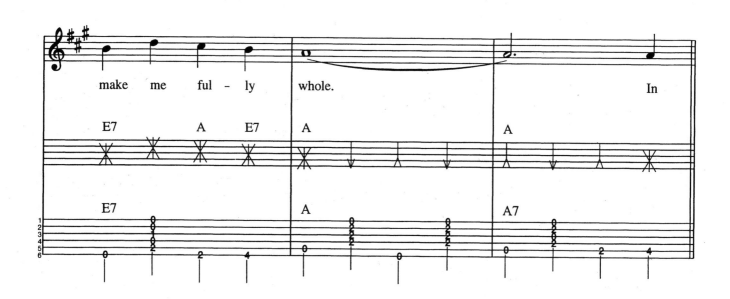

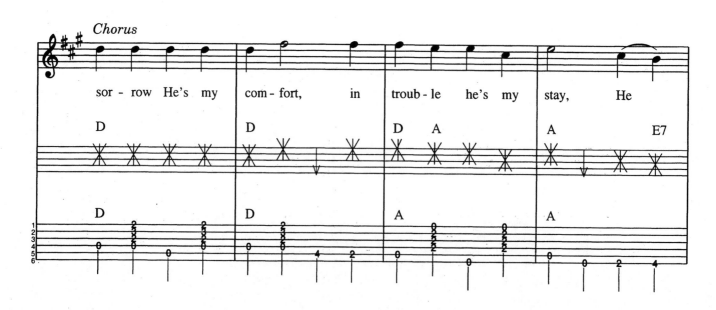

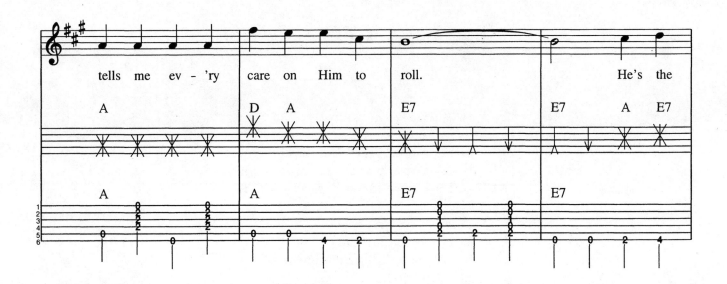

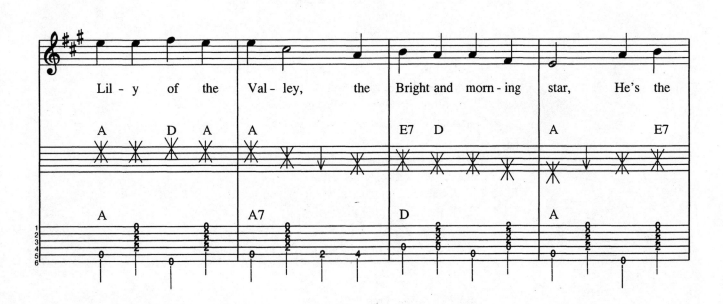

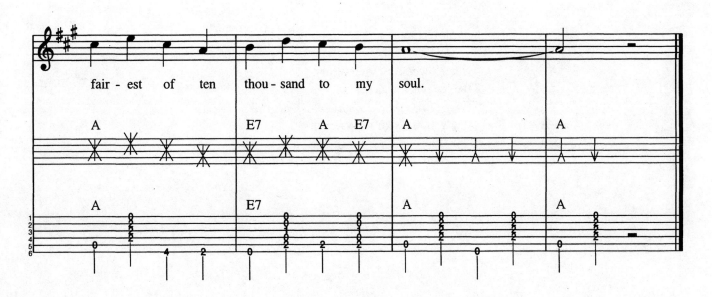

The Lily Of The Valley

1.   I have found a friend in Jesus,
He's ev'rything to me,
He's the fairest of ten
thousand to my soul;
The Lily of the valley,
in Him alone I see all I
need to cleanse and make me fully whole.

In sorrow He's my comfort,
in trouble He's my stay,
He tells me ev'ry care on Him to roll.
He's the Lily of the valley,
the bright and Morning Star,
He's the fairest of ten thousand to my soul.

2.   He all my grief has taken,
and all my sorrows borne;
In temptation He's my strong and mighty tow'r;
I have all for Him forsaken,
and all my idols torn from my heart,
and now he keeps me by His pow'r.

Tho' all the world forsake me,
and Satan tempts me sore,
Thru' Jesus I shall safely reach the goal,
He's the Lily of the valley,
the bright and Morning Star,
He's the fairest of ten thousand to my soul.

3.   He will never, never leave me,
nor yet forsake me here,
While I live by faith and do his blessed will;
A wall of fire about me,
I've nothing now to fear,
with His manner He my hungry soul shall fill.

Then sweeping up to glory,
to see His blessed face,
Where rivers of delight shall ever roll,
He's the Lily of the valley,
the bright and Morning Star,
He's the fairest of ten thousand to my soul.

Where The Soul Never Dies

Wm. M. Golden

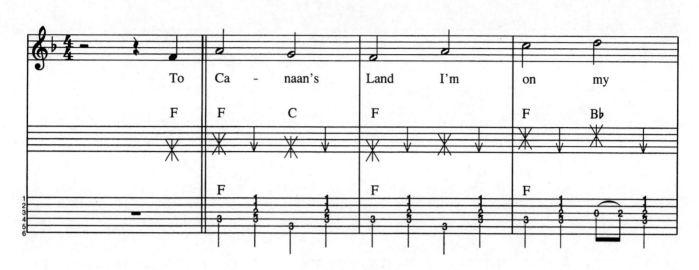

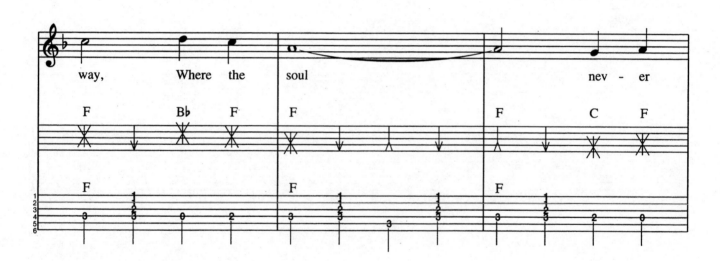

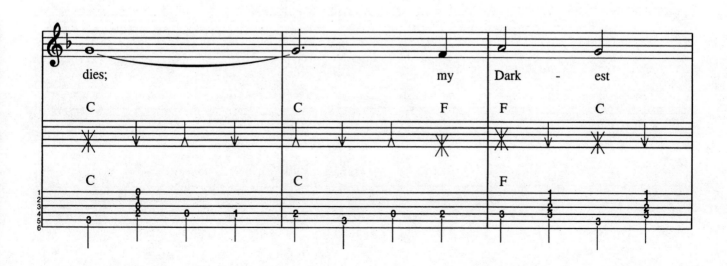

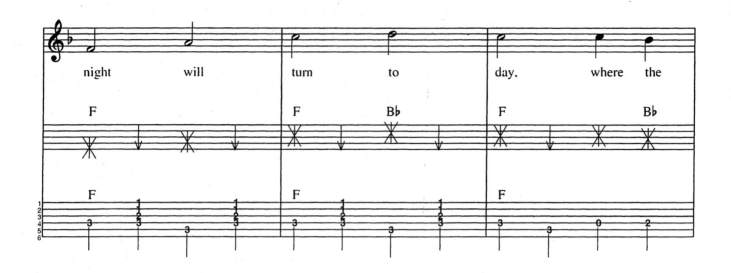

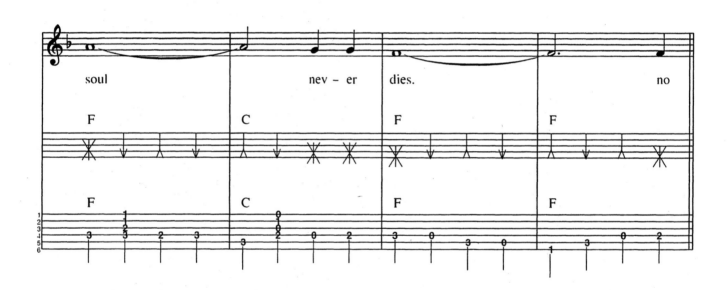

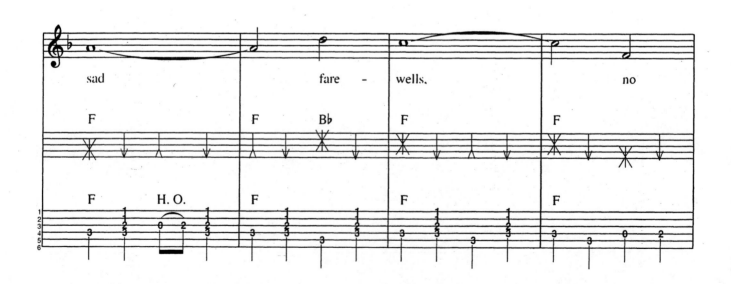

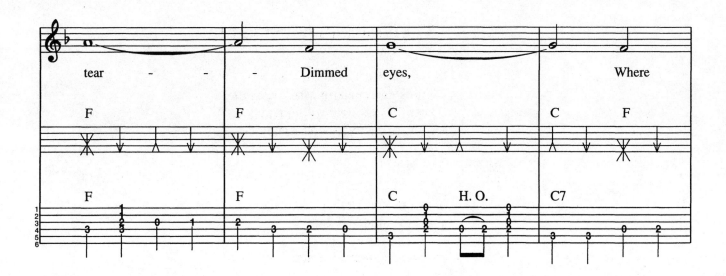

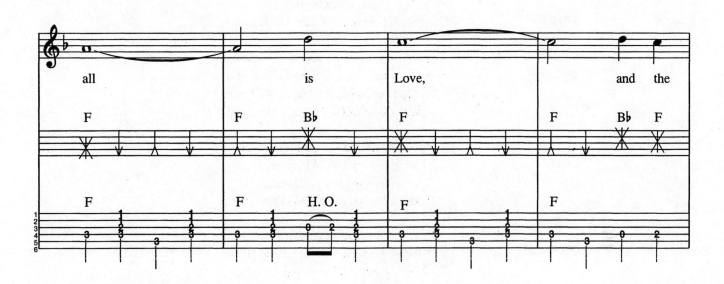

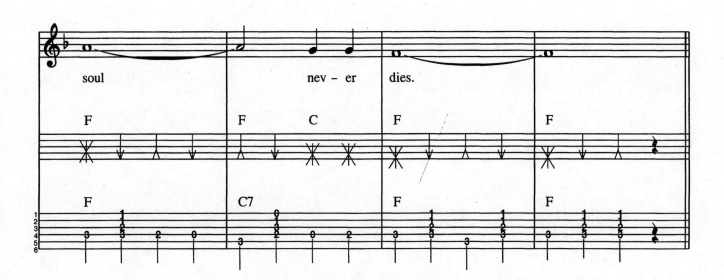

Where The Soul Never Dies

1.   To Canaan's land I'm on my way,
        Where the soul (of Man) never dies;
        My darkest night will turn to day,
        Where the soul (of Man) never dies.

REFRAIN

        No sad farewells,
        no tear dimmed eyes,
        Where all is love,
        Where the soul never dies.

2.   A rose is blooming there for me,
        Where the soul (of Man) never dies;
        And I will spend eternity,
        Where the soul (of Man) never dies.

3.   A love light beams across the foam,
        Where the soul (of Man) never dies;
        It shines to light the shores of home,
        Where the soul (of Man) never dies.

4.   My life will end in deathless sleep,
        Where the soul (of Man) never dies;
        And everlasting joys I'll reap,
        Where the soul (of Man) never dies.

5.   I'm on my way to that fair land,
        Where the soul (of Man) never dies;
        Where there will be no parting hand,
        Where the soul (of Man) never dies.

When The Saints Go Marching In

Arr. by Steve Kaufman

When The Saints Go Marching In

1.   When the sun refuse' to shine,
When the sun refuse' to shine;
Dear Lord I want to be in that number
When the sun refuse' to shine.

REFRAIN

When the saints go marching in,
When the saints go marching in;
Dear Lord I want to be in that number
When the saints go marching in.

2.   When the moon turns into blood,
When the moon turns into blood;
Dear Lord I want to be in that number
When the moon turns into blood.

3.   When we crown Him King of kings,
When we crown Him King of kings;
Dear Lord I want to be in that number
When we crown Him King of kings.

4.   When they gather 'round the throne,
When they gather 'round the throne;
Dear Lord I want to be in that number
When they gather 'round the throne.

5.   While the happy ages roll,
While the happy ages roll;
Dear Lord I want to be in that number
While the happy ages roll.

What A Friend

Charles C. Converse

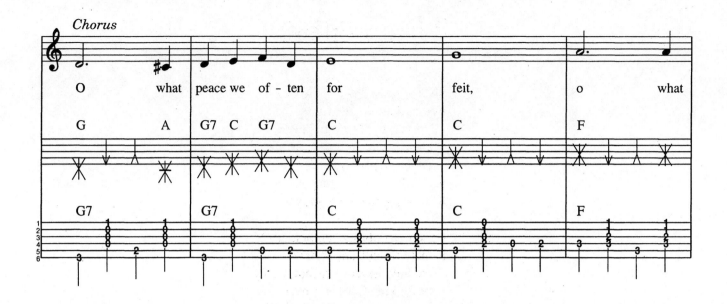

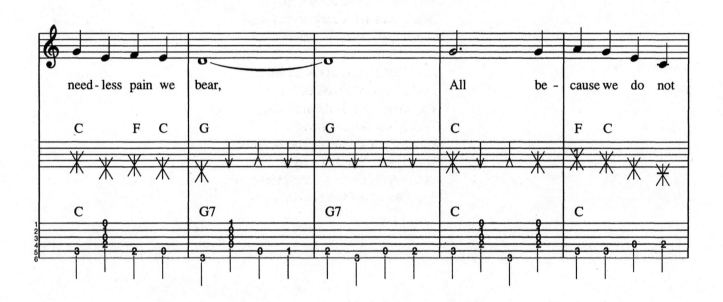

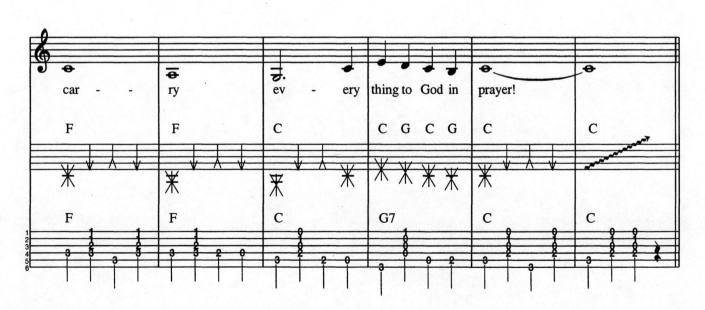

What A Friend

1.   What a friend we have in Jesus,
All our sins and grief to bear!
What a privilege to carry
Everything to God in prayer!
O what peace we often forfeit,
O what needless pain we bear,
All because we do not carry
Everything to God in prayer!

2.   Have we trials and temptations?
Is there trouble anywhere?
We should never be discouraged,
Take it to the Lord in prayer.
Can we find a friend so faithful
Who will all our sorrows share?
Jesus knows our every weakness,
Take it to the Lord in prayer.

3.   Are we weak and heavy laden,
Cumbered with a load of care?
Precious Savior, still our refuge,
Take it the Lord in prayer.
Do thy friends despise, forsake thee?
Take it to the Lord in prayer;
In His arms He'll take and shield thee,
Thou wilt find a solace there.

The Unclouded Day

Rev. J. K. Alwood

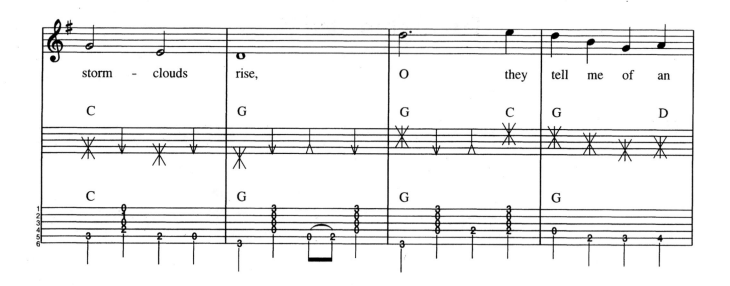

Chorus

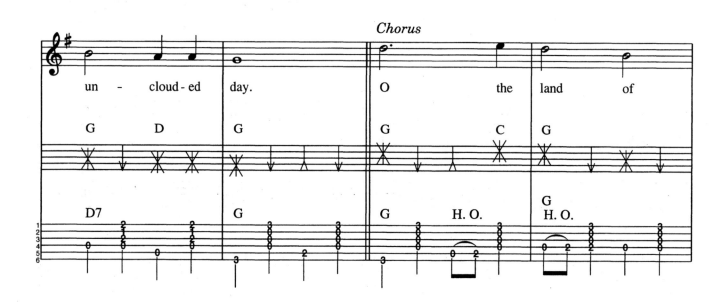

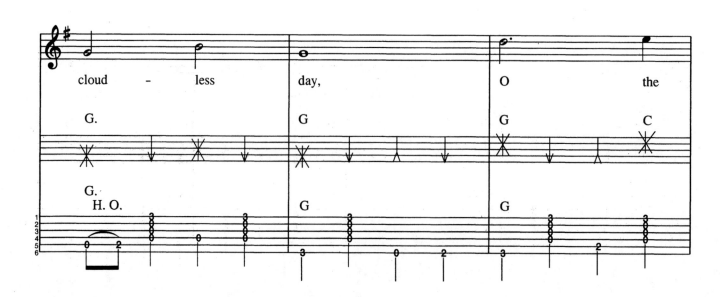

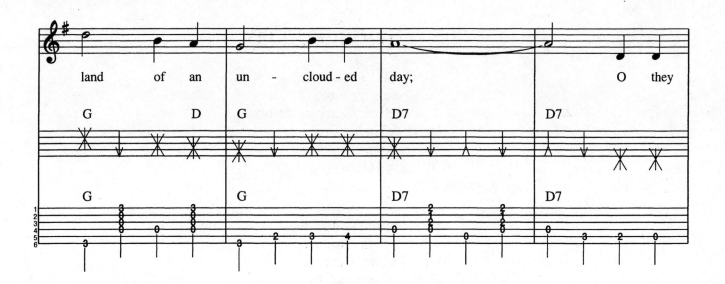

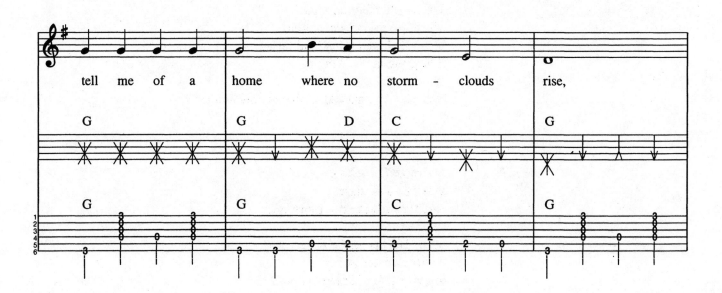

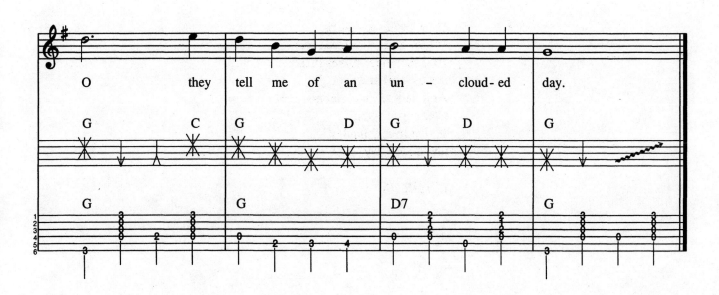

59

The Unclouded Day

1. O they tell me of a home
    far beyond the skies,
    O they tell me of a home far away;
    O they tell me of a home
    where no storm clouds rise
    O, they tell me of an unclouded day.

CHORUS

O the land of cloudless day,
O the land of an unclouded day,
O they tell me of a home
where no storm clouds rise,
O, they tell me of an unclouded day.

2. O they tell me of a home
    where my friends have gone,
    O they tell me of that land far away,
    Where the tree of life
    in eternal bloom
    Sheds its fragrance thro' the unclouded day.

CHORUS

3. O they tell of a King
    in His beauty there,
    And they tell me that mine eyes
    shall behold
    where He sits on the throne that is
    whiter than snow,
    In the city that is made of gold.

CHORUS

4. O they tell me that He
    smiles on His children there,
    And His smile drives their
    sorrows all away;
    And they tell me that no tears
    ever come again,
    In that lovely land of
    unclouded day.

CHORUS

Sweet Hour Of Prayer

Wm. B. Bradbury

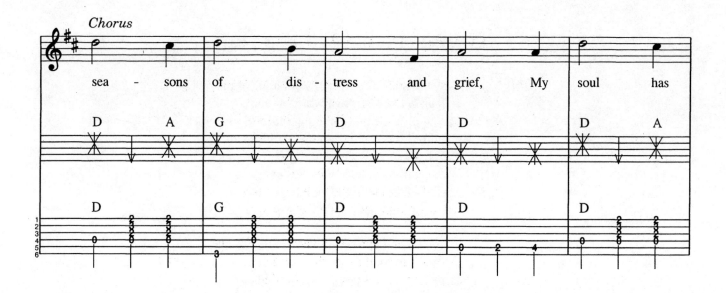

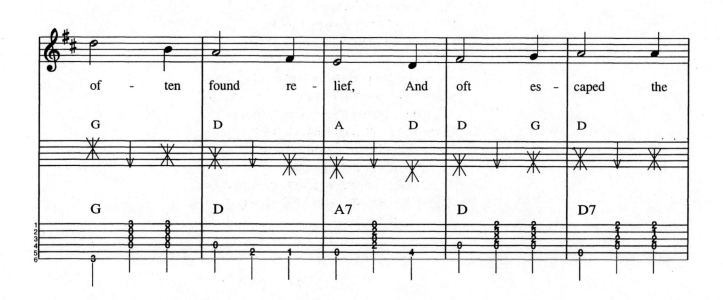

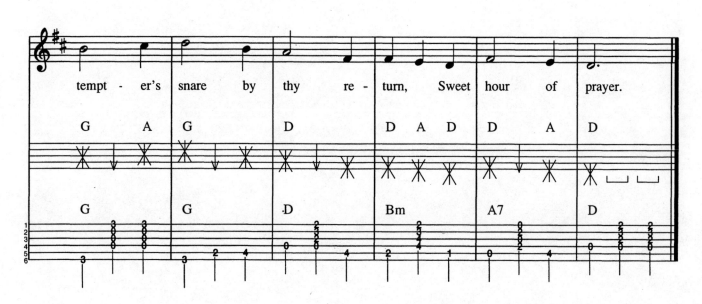

Sweet Hour Of Prayer

1. Sweet hour of prayer! Sweet hour of prayer!
That calls me from a world of care,
And bids me at my Father's throne
Make all my wants and wishes known;
In seasons of distress and grief,
My soul has often found relief,
And oft escaped the tempter's snare
By thy return, sweet hour of prayer.

2. Sweet hour of prayer! Sweet hour of prayer!
Thy wings shall my petition bear
To Him whose truth and faithfulness
Engage the waiting soul to bless;
And since He bids me seek His face,
Believe His Word and trust His Grace,
I'll cast on Him my every care,
And wait for thee, Sweet hour of prayer.

3. Sweet hour of prayer! Sweet hour of prayer!
May I thy consolation share,
Till, from Mount Pisgah's lofty height,
I view my home, and take my flight;
This robe of flesh I'll drop, and rise
To seize the everlasting prize;
And shout, while passing through the air,
Farewell, farewell, sweet hour of prayer.

*This page has been
left blank to avoid
awkward page turns*

Precious Memories

J. B. F. Wright

Chorus

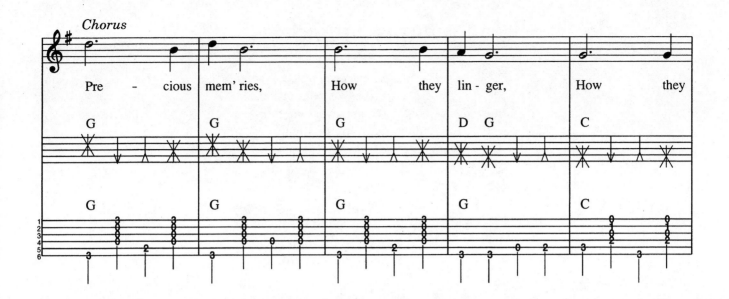

Pre - cious mem' ries, How they lin - ger, How they

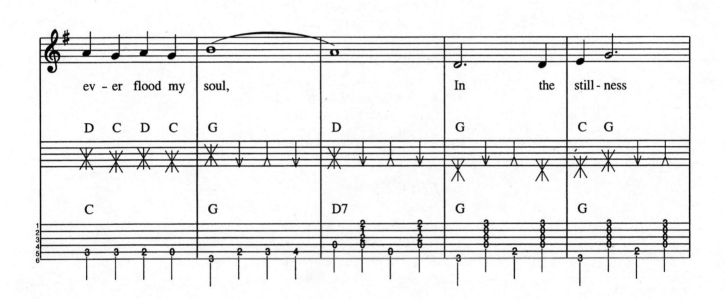

ev - er flood my soul, In the still - ness

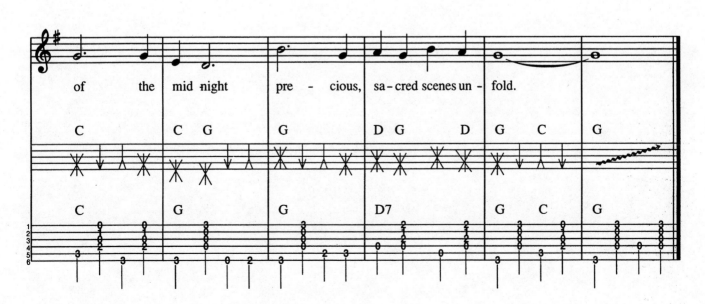

of the mid night pre - cious, sa - cred scenes un - fold.

67

Precious Memories

1. Precious Mem'ries, unseen angels,
   Sent from somewhere to my soul;
   How they linger, ever near me,
   And the sacred past unfold.

REFRAIN

   Precious Mem'ries, how they linger,
   How they ever flood my soul;
   In the stillness of the midnight,
   Precious, sacred scenes unfold.

2. Precious Father, loving mother,
   Fly across the lonely years;
   And old home scenes of my childhood,
   In fond memory appear.

CHORUS

3. In the stillness of the midnight,
   Echoes from the past I hear;
   Old time singing, gladness bringing,
   From that lovely land somewhere.

CHORUS

4. As I travel on life's pathway,
   Know not what the years may hold;
   As I ponder, hope grows fonder,
   Precious memories flood my soul.

CHORUS

*This page has been
left blank to avoid
awkward page turns*

Old Time Religion

Arr. by Steve Kaufman

Old Time Religion

REFRAIN

'Tis the old time religion,
'Tis the old time religion,
'Tis the old time religion,
It's good enough for me.

1.   Makes me love everybody,
Makes me love everybody,
Makes me love everybody,
it's good enough for me.

2.   It was good for our mothers,

3.   It has saved all our fathers,

4.   It will save all our children,

5.   It was good for Paul and Silas,

6.   It will do when I'm dying,

7.   It will take us all to heaven,

The Old Rugged Cross

Rev. Geo. Bennard

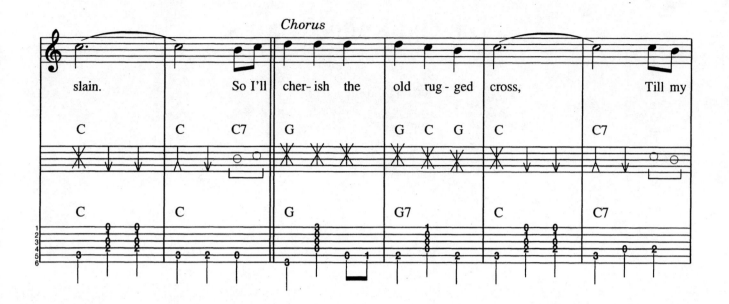

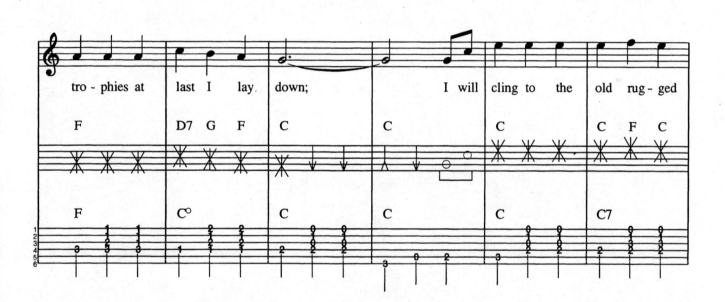

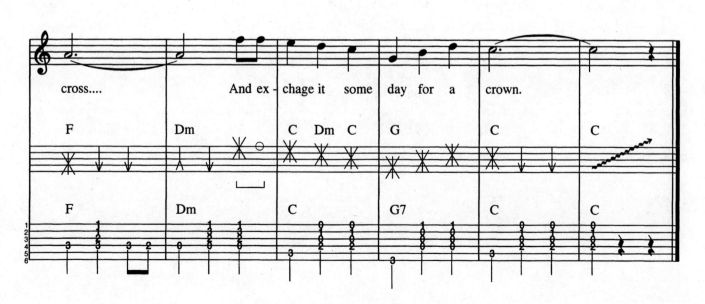

The Old Rugged Cross

1. On a hill far away
   stood an old rugged cross,
   the emblem of suffering and shame;
   And I love that old cross
   where the dearest and best
   for a world of lost sinners was slain.

CHORUS

So I'll cherish the old rugged cross, ...
Till my trophies at last I lay down;
I will cling to the old rugged cross, ...
And exchange it some day for a crown.

2. Oh, that old rugged cross,
   so despised by the world,
   has a wondrous attraction for me;
   For the dear Lamb of God
   left His glory above,
   to bear it to dark Calvary.

CHORUS

3. In the old rugged cross,
   stained with blood so divine,
   a wondrous beauty I see;
   For 'twas on that old cross
   Jesus suffered and died,
   to pardon and sanctify me.

CHORUS

4. To the old rugged cross
   I will ever be true,
   Its shame and reproach gladly bear;
   Then He'll call me someday
   to my home far away,
   where His glory forever I'll share.

CHORUS

The Old Gospel Ship

Arr. by Steve Kaufman

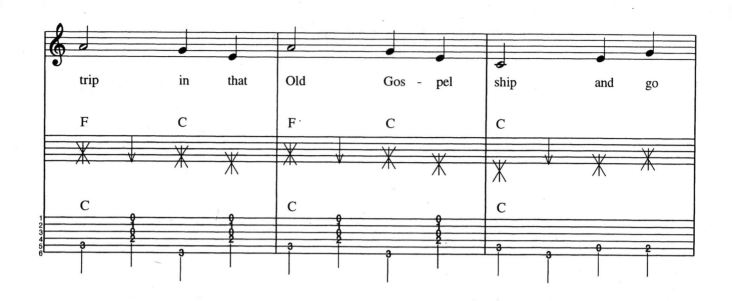

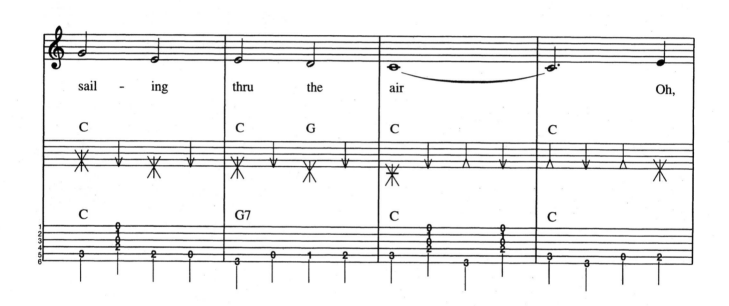

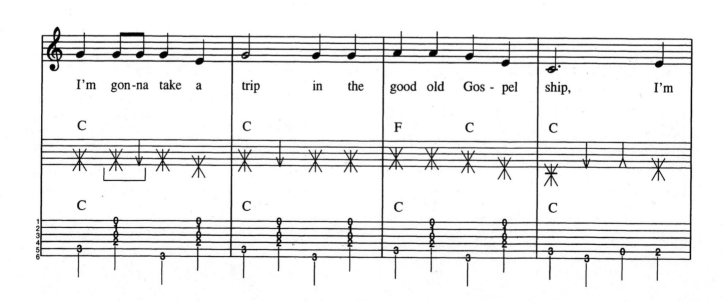

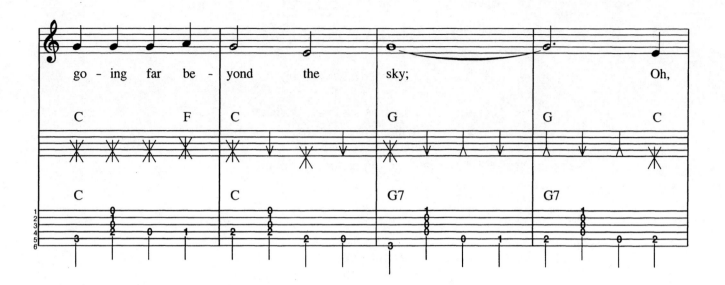

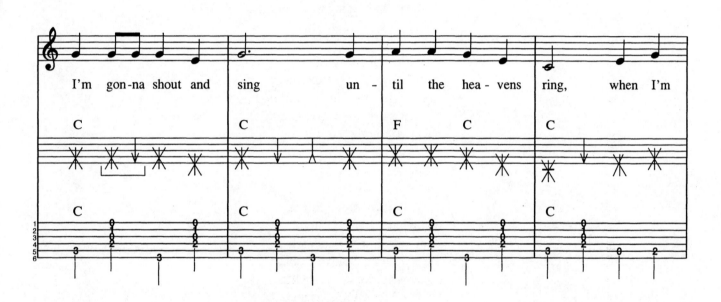

The Old Gospel Ship

1.   I have good news to bring,
   and that is why I sing,
   all my joys with you I'll share;
   I'm going to take a trip,
   in that Old Gospel ship,
   and go sailing through the air.

CHORUS

        Oh, I'm "gonna" take a trip,
in that old gospel ship,
I'm going far beyond the sky;
Oh, I'm "gonna" shout and sing,
until the heavens ring,
when I'm bidding this world good-bye.

2.   Oh, I can scarcely wait,
   I know I'll not be late,
   for I'll spend my time in pray'r;
   And when my ship comes in,
   I will leave this world of sin,
   and go sailing through the air.

CHORUS

3.   If you're ashamed of me,
   you have no cause to be,
   for with Christ I am an heir;
   If too much fault you find,
   you will sure be left behind,
   while I go sailing through the air.

CHORUS

Sweet By and By

J. P. Webster

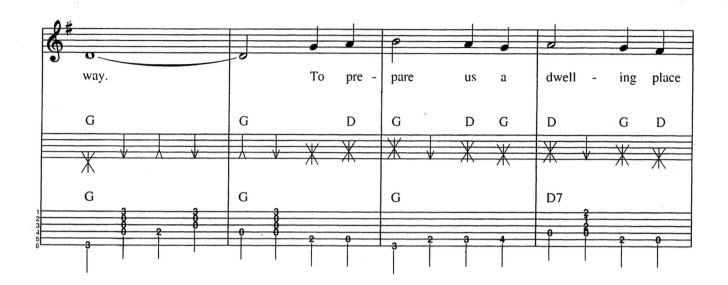

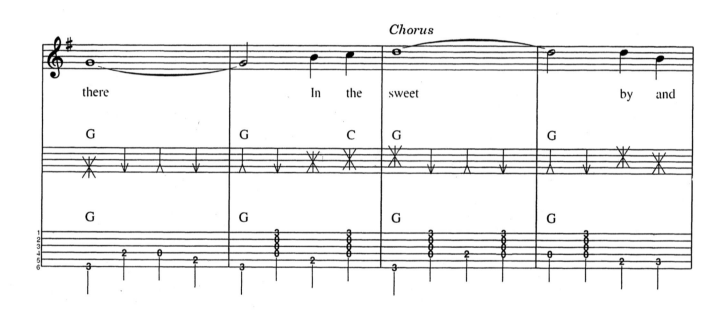

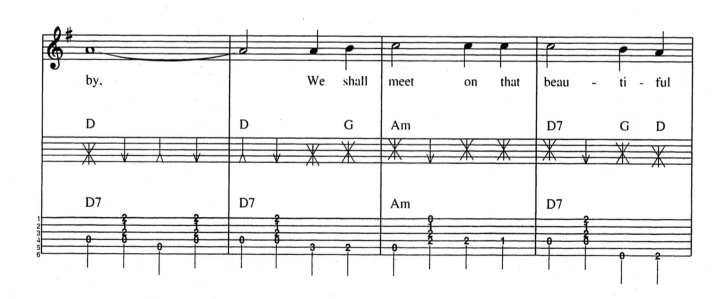

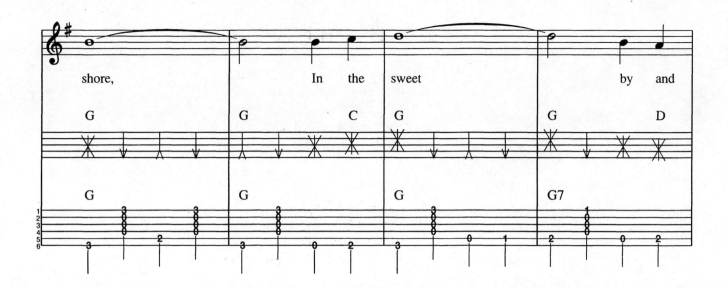

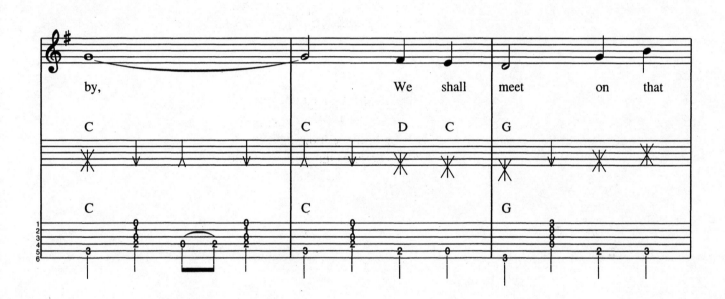

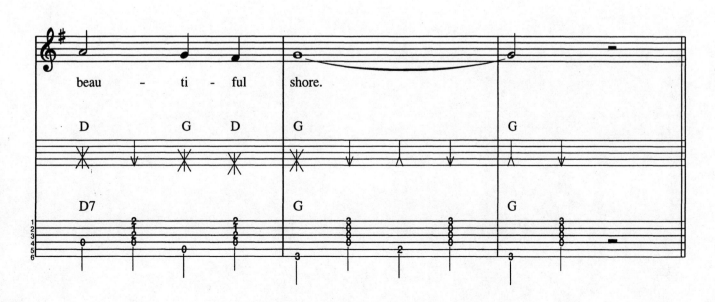

Sweet By And By

1. There's a land that is fairer than day,
   and by faith we can see it afar;
   For the Father waits over the way,
   to prepare us a dwelling place there.

CHORUS

In the sweet by and by,
we shall meet on that beautiful shore;
In the sweet by and by,
we shall meet on that beautiful shore.

2. We shall sing on that beautiful shore,
   the melodious songs of the blest;
   And our spirits shall sorrow no more,
   Not a sigh for the blessing of rest.

CHORUS

3. To the bountiful Father above,
   we will offer our tribute of praise;
   For the glorious gift of His love,
   and the blessings that hallow our days.

CHORUS

Heaven's Jubilee

G. T. Speer

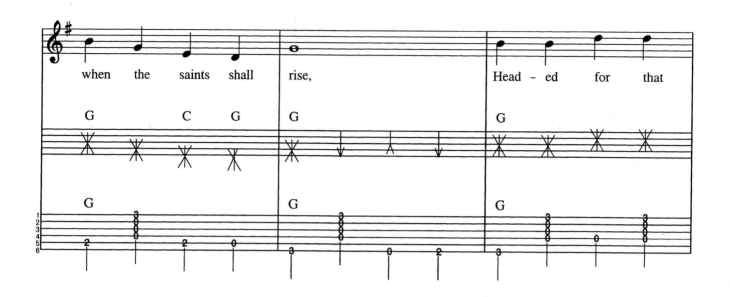

when the saints shall rise, Head – ed for that

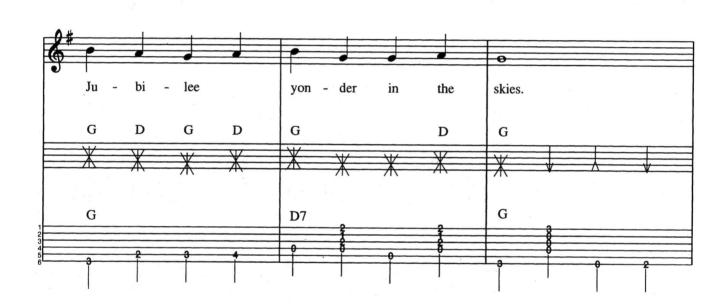

Ju – bi – lee yon – der in the skies.

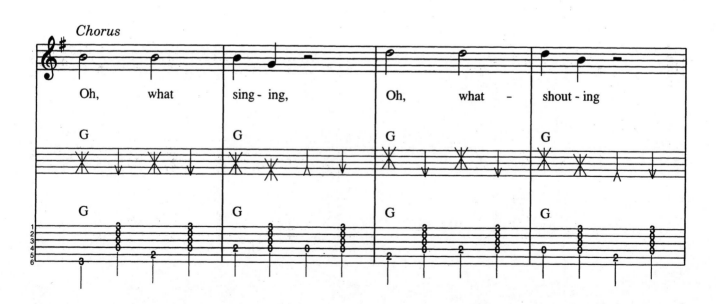

Chorus

Oh, what sing – ing, Oh, what – shout – ing

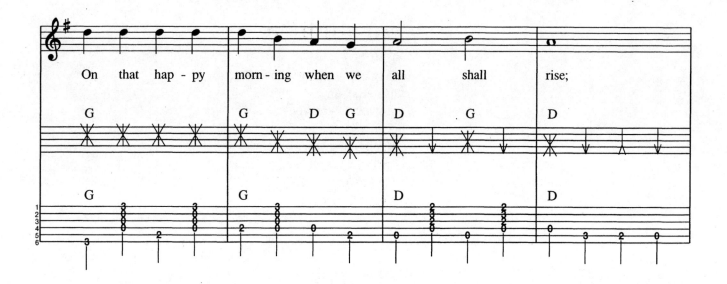

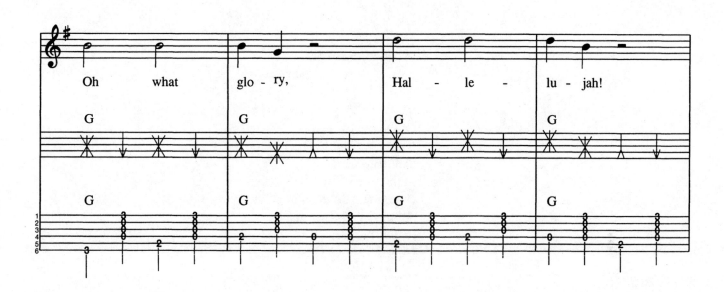

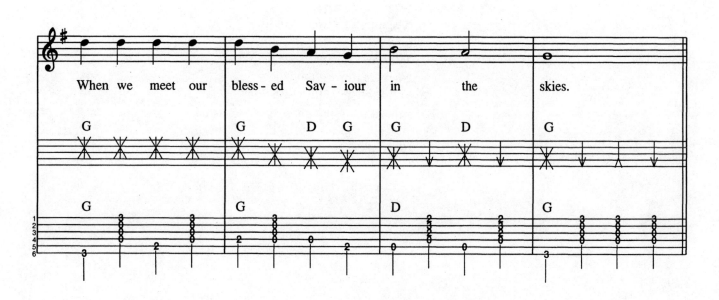

Heaven's Jubilee

1.   Some glad morning we shall see
Jesus in the air,
Coming after you and me
Joy is ours to share;
What rejoicing there will be
when the saints shall rise,
Headed for that Jubilee,
yonder in the skies.

CHORUS

Oh, what singing;
oh, what shouting,
on that happy morning
when we all shall rise;
Oh, what glory,
Hallelujah!
When we meet our
blessed Savior in the skies.

2.   Seems that now I almost see
all the sainted dead,
Rising for that Jubilee,
that is just ahead;
In the twinkling of an eye
changing with them to be,
All the living saints to fly
to that Jubilee.

CHORUS

3.   When with all the heav'nly host
we begin to sing,
Singing in the Holy Ghost,
how the heav'ns will ring;
Millions there will join the song,
when them we shall be,
Praising Christ thru ages long,
heaven's Jubilee.

CHORUS

*This page has been
left blank to avoid
awkward page turns*

Just A Closer Walk With Thee

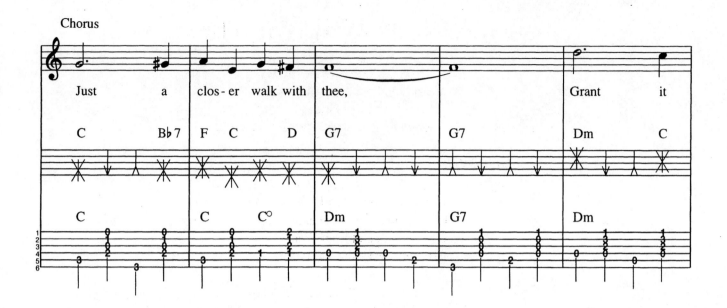

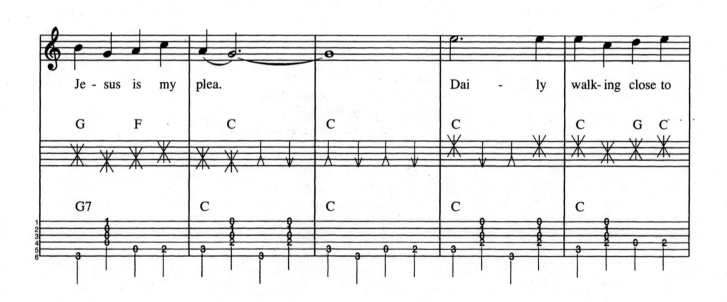

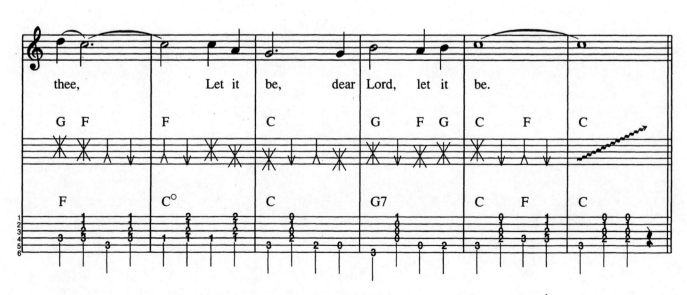

89

Just A Closer Walk With Thee

1.   I am weak, but thou art strong,
              Jesus keep me from all wrong;
              I'll be satisfied as long,
              as I walk, let me walk, close to Thee.

CHORUS

        Just a closer walk with Thee,
        Grant it Jesus, is my plea;
        Daily walking close to Thee,
        Let it be, dear Lord, let it be.

2.   Thru this world of toils and snares,
              if I falter Lord, who cares;
              Who with me my burden shares?
              None but Thee, dear Lord, none by Thee.

CHORUS

3.   When my feeble life is o'er,
              time for me will be no more;
              Guide me gently, safely o'er,
              to my home on the bright golden shore.

CHORUS

4.   When life's sun sets in the west,
              Lord may I have done my best;
              May I find sweet peace and rest,
              in that home, happy home, of the blest.

CHORUS

*This page has been
left blank to avoid
awkward page turns*

In The Garden

C. Austin Miles

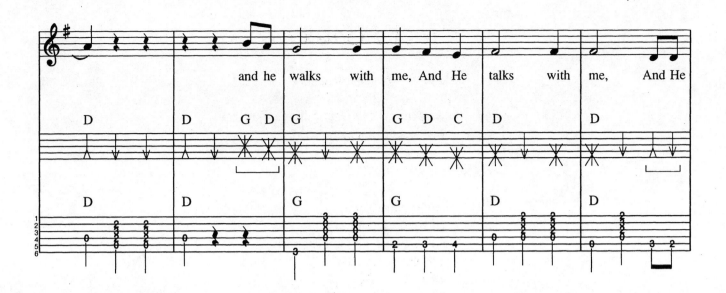

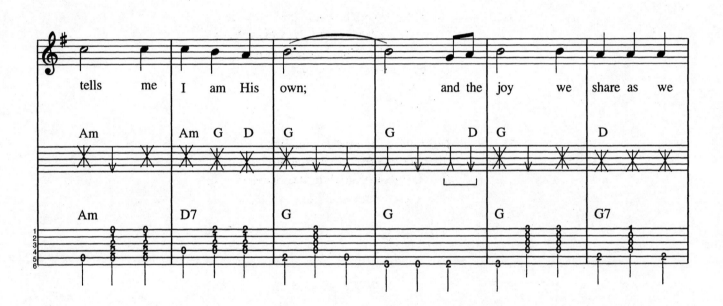

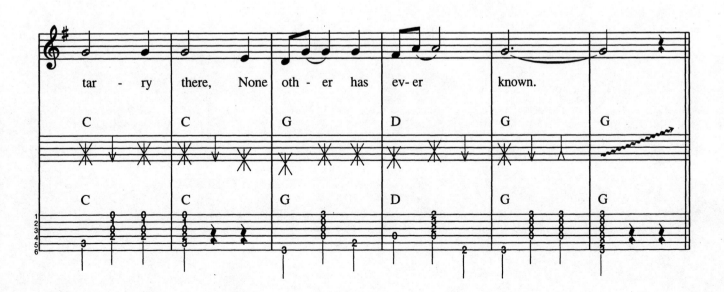

In The Garden

1.   I come to the garden alone,
   while dew is still on the roses;
   And the voice I hear, falling on my ear,
   the Son of God discloses.

CHORUS

And he walks with me,
and he talks with me,
and He tells me I am His own;
And the joy we share,
as we tarry there,
none other has ever known.

2.   He speaks, and the sound of His voice
   is sweet and the birds hush their singing;
   And the melody that He gave to me,
   within my heart is ringing.

CHORUS

3.   I'd stay in the garden with Him,
   though the night around me be falling;
   But he bids me go, thru' the voice of woe,
   His voice to me is calling

CHORUS

A Beautiful Life

Wm. M. Golden

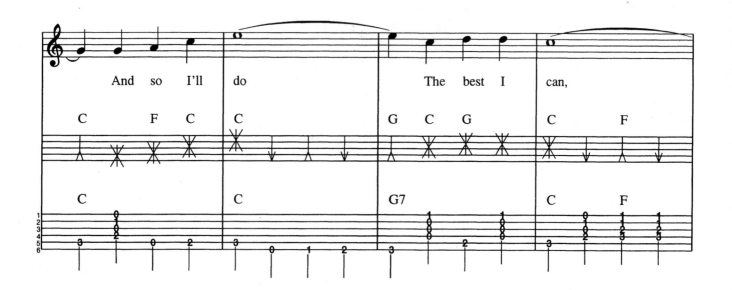

And so I'll do   The best I can,

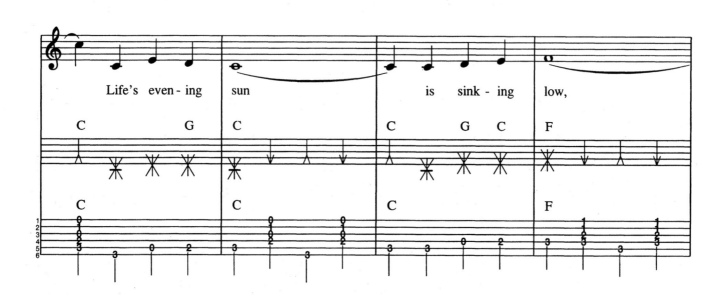

Life's even-ing sun   is sink-ing low,

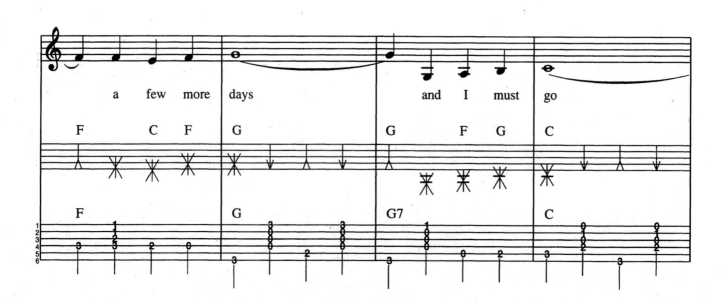

a few more days   and I must go

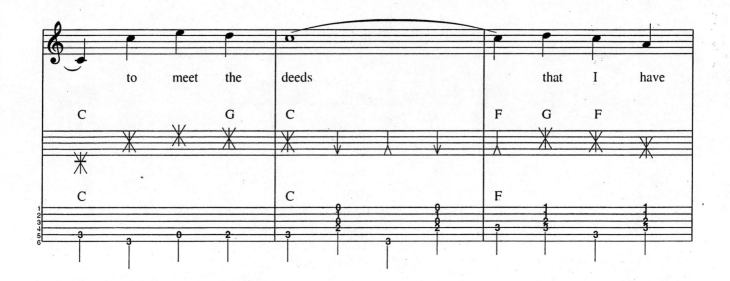

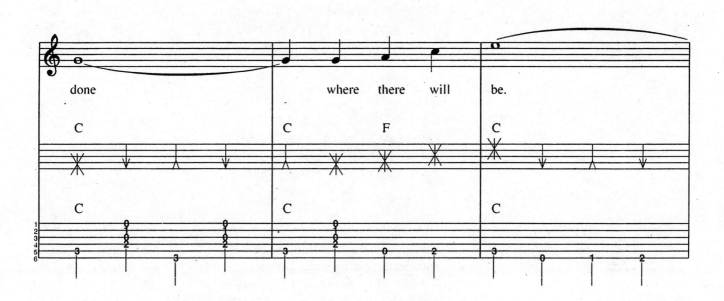

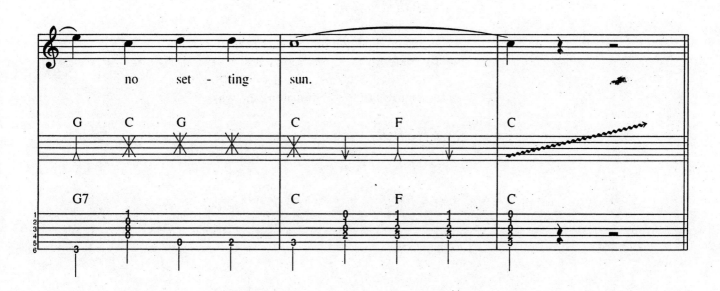

A Beautiful Life

1.   Each day I'll do a golden deed,
by helping those who are in need;
My life on earth is but a span,
and so I'll do the best I can.

CHORUS

Life's evening sun is sinking low,
a few more days and I must go;
To meet the deeds that I have done,
where there will be no setting sun.

2.   To be a child of God each day,
my light must shine along the way;
I'll sing His praise while ages roll,
and strive to help some troubled soul.

CHORUS

3.   The only life that will endure,
is one that's kind and good and pure;
And so for God I'll take my stand,
Each day I'll lend a helping hand.

CHORUS

4.   I'll help some one in time of need,
and journey on with rapid speed;
I'll help the sick, the poor and weak,
and words of kindness to them speak.

CHORUS

5.   While going down life's weary road,
I'll try to lift some trav'ler's load;
I'll try to turn the night to day,
and make flowers bloom along the way.

CHORUS

There Is Power In The Blood

Lewis E. Jones

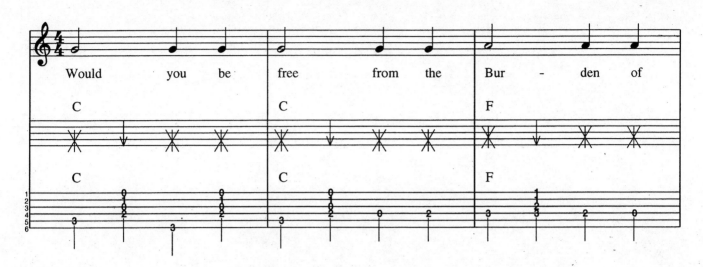

Would you be free from the Bur - den of

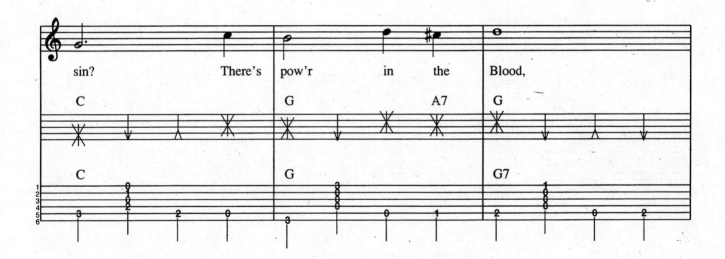

sin? There's pow'r in the Blood,

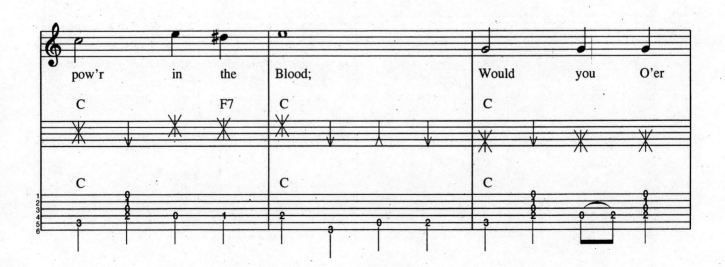

pow'r in the Blood; Would you O'er

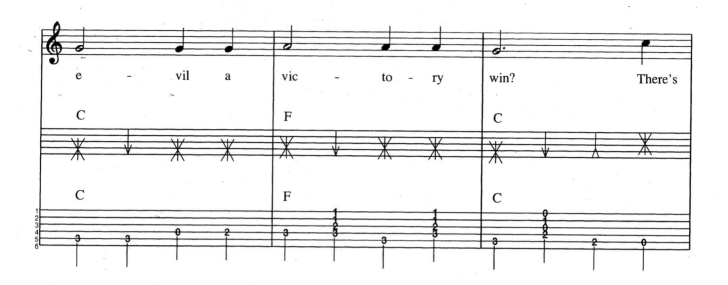

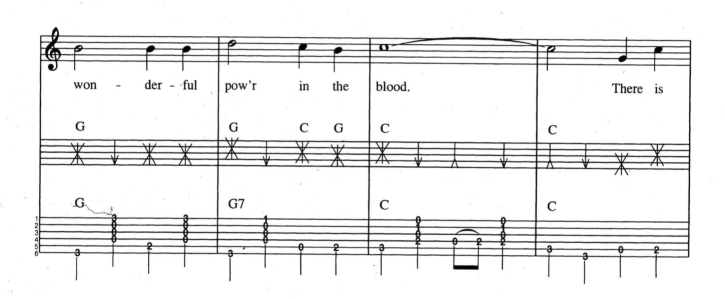

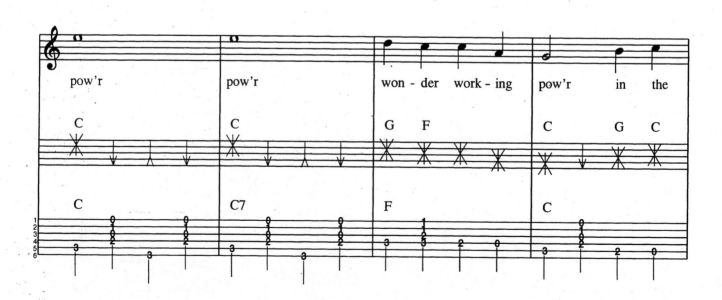

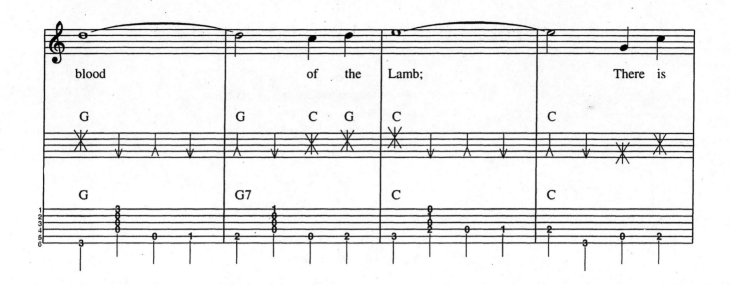

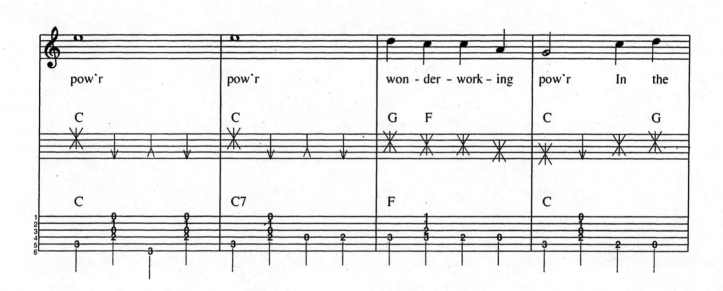

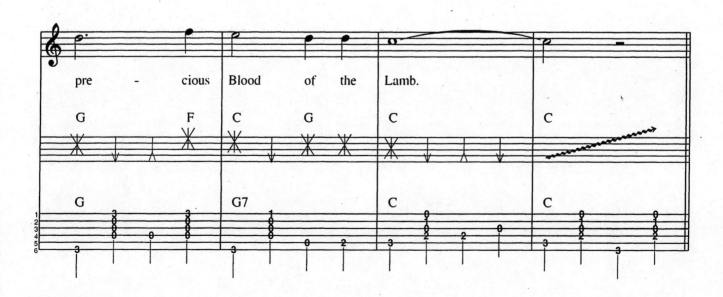

There Is Power In The Blood

1.   Would you be free from the burden of Sin?
There's pow'r in the blood, pow'r in the blood;
Would you o'er evil a victory win?
There's wonderful pow'r in the blood.

CHORUS

There is pow'r, pow'r, wonder working pow'r
In the blood of the lamb;
There is pow'r, pow'r, wonder working pow'r
In the precious blood of the lamb.

2.   Would you be free from your passion and pride?
There's pow'r in the blood, pow'r in the blood;
Come for cleansing to Calvary's tide?
There's wonderful pow'r in the blood.

CHORUS

3.   Would you be whiter, much whiter than snow?
There's pow'r in the blood, pow'r in the blood;
Sin stains are lost in its life-giving flow,
There's wonderful pow'r in the blood.

CHORUS

4.   Would you do service for Jesus your King?
There's pow'r in the blood, pow'r in the blood;
Would you live daily His praises to sing?
There's wonderful pow'r in the blood.

CHORUS

Great Music at Your Fingertips